ASTRONAUT
GODS
OF THE MAYA

ASTRONAUT
GODS
OF THE MAYA

Extraterrestrial Technologies in
the **Temples** and **Sculptures**

ERICH von DÄNIKEN

Translated by Aida Sefic Williams

Bear & Company
Rochester, Vermont • Toronto, Canada

Bear & Company
One Park Street
Rochester, Vermont 05767
www.BearandCompanyBooks.com

Bear & Company is a division of Inner Traditions International

Originally published in 2011 in German under the title *Was ist falsch im Maya-Land?: Versteckte Technologien in Tempeln und Skulpturen* by Kopp Verlag
First U.S. edition published in 2017 by Bear & Company

Library of Congress Cataloging-in-Publication Data
Names: Däniken, Erich von, 1935- author.
Title: Astronaut gods of the Maya : extraterrestrial technologies in the temples and
    sculptures / Erich von Däniken.
Other titles: Was ist falsch im Maya-Land? English
Description: Rochester, Vermont : Bear & Company, 2017. | Includes bibliographical
    references and index.
Identifiers: LCCN 2016048809 (print) | LCCN 2017013672 (e-book) |
    ISBN 9781591432357 (pbk.) | ISBN 9781591432364 (e-book)
Subjects: LCSH: Mayas—Extraterrestrial influences. | Mayas—Antiquities. |
Mayas—Religion. | Extraterrestrial beings—Central America—History—
    To 1500. | Technology—Central America—History—To 1500. | Temples—
    Central America. | Maya sculpture. | Central America—Antiquities.
Classification: LCC F1435.3.E87 D36 2017 (print) | LCC F1435.3.E87 (e-book) |
    DDC 001.942—dc23
LC record available at https://lccn.loc.gov/2016048809

Printed and bound in India by Replika Press Pvt. Ltd.

10 9 8 7 6 5 4 3 2 1

Text design by Virginia Scott Bowman and layout by Debbie Glogover
This book was typeset in Garamond Premier Pro with Hypatia Sans Pro and Helvetica
Neue LT Std as display fonts

Cover images courtesy of IngImage

To send correspondence to the author of this book, mail a first-class letter to the author c/o Inner Traditions • Bear & Company, One Park Street, Rochester, VT 05767, and we will forward the communication, or contact the author directly at **www.daniken.com**.

CONTENTS

Figure 1

Letter to My Readers

Dear Reader,

This book is like a journey through time. In text and image, I want to document that among the Maya and Aztec not everything is, by a long shot, what we have been taught—another way of looking yields a new result.

The chaos had already begun with Christopher Columbus. On October 12, 1492, his son wrote in his diary: "We noticed two or three settlements, and the native people called to us and thanked God. Some brought water, others brought something to eat. . . . They asked us if we came from heaven."[1]

The bewildered and utterly baffled natives did not suspect what actually had occurred. Soon after the first encounter, coffee-brown, stark-naked natives ran from all heavenly directions to the landing site and were part of an incomprehensible ceremony. Columbus, as well as the captains and officers of the accompanying ships *Pinta* and *Nina,* wore ostentatious garments: dark-brown and dark-red velvet costumes with white Flemish ruffs; Turkish trousers and wide, silver-studded belts; violet silk stockings; and on top of it all, the coats of the Spanish court cavalry. Columbus himself, as has been documented, wore a wide hat from which gold coins jingled. In one hand he carried his rapier and the royal flag in the other. The escorting officers waved flags. Next, two bearded monks in brown cowls tramped over the planking, with a cross on their shoulders. Finally, another part of the ship's crew was added, coarse swashbucklers in multicolored clothes. Then bald-headed men staggered ashore, but the Indians were not familiar with bald people. Some had shoes, others were barefoot, and some of the foul-smelling mates wore brightly colored shirts. Still others, despite the humid heat, wore iron helmets. And naturally they carried their knives, rapiers, and shotguns—verily, they made a scintillating and estimable bunch.

Looking back, it's amazing that, confronted with this otherworldly theater troupe, the native inhabitants did not run away as if from the devil.

Columbus and his officers generously gave out gifts: cheap red caps, worthless glass pearls, kitschy small mirrors, and some hair combs. The natives reverently named these trifles *turey*. That means "heaven."

A convincing example of magic, with which Columbus fooled the natives, occurred on December 26, 1492. Columbus demonstrated his "godly" power: "I fired a bombard [heavy piece of artillery] and a shotgun. As the Indians heard the crash and saw the muzzle flash, they threw themselves on the ground. It took a long time until they dared to move again."[2]

Almost thirty years later, in 1519, this inglorious play was repeated in a dramatic fashion. Hernando Cortez turned up off the coast of Mexico with eleven ships, 100 sailors, and 508 soldiers. Cortez wanted to command respect and let a cannonball fly over the heads of the Indians. He noted that the natives fell to the ground as if they were dead, and they lay terrified for a while.

Francisco Pizarro was at first classified as a god by the Incas in South America.[3] And the British Captain Cook, who discovered the South Sea Islands, had the same experience: the natives considered him the returned god Rongo, or Longo[4] (figure 1, page vi).

A little pageantry, a little noise, a little superior technology, and any hillbilly would cower in fear.

Today we would say that the indigenous tribes were overwhelmed. They did not know the technologies of the conquerors. They could not classify the foreign beings, uniforms, and weapons. And so the conquerors grew into gods in the imagination of the natives. We all know these were no gods and they never were. The term "gods" resulted from a misunderstanding.

All this happened centuries ago, and something like that could not happen again.

Really?

An example familiar from Christianity verifies our distorted view: Everyone certainly knows that Jesus of Nazareth preached in Palestine 2,000 years ago and was finally executed by the Romans. For this, there is the written testimony of the Gospels and letters of the apostles. Christianity spread to many corners of the world; a hundred thousand chapels, churches, and wonderful cathedrals were built. In them one can find altars with grandiose oil paintings, Christian artwork made of gold and silver, statues of the Virgin Mary, and crucifixion scenes. A Christian culture was created with its own music, such as Gregorian chants or the orchestral masses of Johann Sebastian Bach.

Have you ever thought that of all those artists and composers who placed their creativity in the service of religion none were eyewitnesses to the actual events? No architects of any cathedral or church, no masons of stone altars, no crib carver of Oberammergau observed the birth and the life of Jesus with his own eyes. Neither Michelangelo nor Bach was present for the Last Supper, and no artisans of the past 2,000 years heard the Sermon on the Mount "live." All of them—without exception—became tools of tradition.

Jesus himself didn't leave behind a single object that could be admired in any museum in the world. He didn't scribble on a single scrap of parchment, press his godly feet in clay, or leave behind his autograph with the actual date of the Roman calendar.

Suppose, in a thousand years, archaeologists were to dig up the remains of Christian churches. With very precise dating they would say that over a period of at least 2,000 years the same motifs were used again and again. They would consistently find crucifixion scenes, manger birth, angels, and apostles with halos on their venerable heads. Naturally, specialist scholars of the future would find contradictions. A Mother of Christ figure from Bavaria will not look the same as a Mother of Christ figure from Kenya. The cathedral of Chartres in France, with its unparalleled beautiful glass windows and its grandiose architecture, is not comparable with the simple concrete churches of 2010. The artists and architects all meant the same thing, but they expressed it in different ways. And something else: due to the discoveries, archaeologists would arrive at the opinion that Jesus of Nazareth changed the earth approximately 2,000 years ago, because the cultural monuments can be dated back to 2,000 years ago.

Those who are Christians know how all of this came about. Will people know this in 1,000 years? How little people know and how quickly misunderstandings arise can be proven from the Age of Discovery. That is exactly what this book is all about. To see the old images in a new light, I must first—willingly or reluctantly—explain for the umpteenth time what ethnologists understand by the term "cargo cult." Without this explanation, some readers will not be able to follow my thinking.

Yours,

Erich von Däniken

July, 2011

Figure 2

Figure 3

Cargo Cults
with Consequences

In the spring of 1945 the Americans built a base camp in the area of Hollandia in New Guinea. At times as many as 40,000 soldiers were stationed there. Airplanes landed and took off nonstop in order to bring supplies for the War of the Pacific. The bush residents, mostly Papuans, observed uncomprehendingly the hustle and bustle of the foreigners. They understood neither world politics nor technology. Now, American soldiers handed out small gifts, such as chocolate, chewing gum, old shoes, or an empty bottle. Soon, the natives described all of these gifts with the word "cargo," a word they had heard from the foreigners. An increasing number of natives ventured out of the bush and to the edges of the airstrip. There, they observed how large silver birds making loud noises rose into the clouds. Possibly to heaven. The natives wished that these heavenly birds would fly directly to their tribal area and there unload their "cargo." What was to be done?[1]

The Papuans believed that they should behave just like the foreigners. So on Wewak Island there was a full makeshift airport with imitation runways and airplanes made of wood and straw (figures 2 and 3). In the eastern highlands of New Guinea, Dutch officers found "radio stations" and "insulators" made out of leaves rolled together (figures 4 and 5). Imitation watches were made out

1

Figure 4

Figure 5

Figure 6

of wood and iron, and imitation steel helmets were made out of tortoise shells. Dutch and American officers observed this tomfoolery, were stunned, and often laughed about it. "With an unbelievable seriousness, the natives bravely imitated everything they observed."[2]

There is also the experience of the German aircraft researcher Hans Bertram when he had to make an emergency landing in Australia. He was not killed by the Aborigines only because he wore aviator goggles. They only knew goggle-like objects from their rock drawings. There, however, those drawings represented the goddess Wandina (figure 6).

As Frank Hurley arrived in the Kaimari village in New Guinea in the 1920s, the natives saw his water plane as a divine bird. Every night, they rowed in a canoe to the bow of the airplane and offered a pig there (figure 7).[3] In ethnology all of these misunderstandings are described with the little term "cargo cult."

Figure 7

The starting point for a cargo cult is always the collision of two different cultures. One culture is technologically less developed than the other and does not understand the technology of the more-developed society (figure 8). All contact between natives and those with superior technologies played out in the same way:

1. The carriers of the superior technologies were seen as "supernatural."
2. The error was soon discovered, and the "supernatural" are brought back into the realm of humans.
3. After meeting the foreigners, others were in turn branded as "supernatural gods." Their return was generally awaited.

Today, we can only chuckle at the reaction of the natives. We think we know better. Indeed, a technologically more advanced culture—such as an extraterrestrial one—would also be assessed by us as supernatural. We would understand their weapons and communication systems as little as the natives understood Columbus and his theater troupe. We would classify technology that is a generation ahead of ours as "magical." Not unlike then. Exactly such misunderstandings are what I want to uncover in this book and expose these cargo cults that we have hitherto attributed to holy goings-on and about which correspondingly profound treatises on religious psychology have been written. I question these seemingly sure assessments—but without the insistence of being right.

Figure 8

Figure 9

The ruins of Tikal lie in current-day Guatemala; its beginnings go back to approximately 1000 BCE. (Remember that ancient Rome was supposedly founded in 753 BCE.) In the center zone of Tikal alone, three thousand buildings are located: houses, palaces, administration buildings, terraces, platforms, pyramids, and altars. What was the purpose of the pyramids? Were they observatories? Why were so many of them crowded so closely together (figures 9 and 10).

Were they graves? To this day, no tombs have been found under the pyramids.

Figure 10

Figure 11

Were the pyramids schools for different ways of thinking? Where would the teachers have taught and the students learned? There is very little room on a pyramid platform (figures 11 and 12).

Were the pyramids sacrificial sites? Not in Tikal, as human sacrifices were not offered until later.

Or were the pyramids possibly memorials of the ruling families? But that doesn't make sense, because different pyramids were erected at the same time. The rulers would have prevented this.

Figure 12

The region under the administration of the Guatemalan government as a national archaeological park consists of an area encompassing 576 square kilometers (222 sq. mi.). This giant area was once the space for a collection of tremendous buildings—currently overgrown by the jungle (figures 13 and 14). Moreover, Tikal lies in an impossible location: there is practically no water. Rulers always sought a site with water for their people. Literally nothing for humans works without water. But in Tikal there was neither creek nor river. The nearest water—Lake Petén Itzá—is 40 kilometers (25 mi.) away. So the Maya dug kilometer-long canals, creating massive water-storage capacity in Tikal, with seven canals located in the inner zone and three in the outer. Radar images have brought to the fore the veins of the irrigation system, which expanded over the entire Yucatán Peninsula.

Figure 13

Figure 14

But why did people erect impressive buildings (figures 15 to 17), made up of millions of stones, in a place without water? This indispensible water must have been available at the groundbreaking. Who carved the stones, carried the stones, piled the stones on top of each other, brought water? The architects in Tikal planned well, because the site was 40 kilometers away from Lake Petén Itzá. Why in the world did it have to be located in this impossible location? What would have been the compelling reason for this?

Figure 15

Figure 16

Figure 17

The same phenomenon also exists in our time. Pilgrimage sites such as Lourdes in southern France, Fátima in Portugal, or Guadalupe in Mexico were created for a single reason: something supernatural occurred there. In Lourdes a girl named Bernadette Soubirous claims far and wide that she saw the Virgin Mother in some rocks (figure 18). In Fátima there were three children who for months saw a white lady in a treetop at the same time on the same day of the month (figure 19). The vision spoke to the children. It was the same in Mexico. There the "Queen of Heaven" came to a young Indian. The ground became sacred. An increasing number of people flocked to the sites of these visions. At first a few candles and some flowers were placed at the sites, and soon there was a chapel, then a church, and finally a cathedral. Hotdog vendors and taverns set up shop, the first hotels were opened. Lourdes, Fátima, Guadalupe, and other sites became places of pilgrimage for many. In Guadalupe, the believers worshipped a

Figure 18

Figure 19

NON FECIT TALITER OMNI NATIONI.

Tocada á su Santissimo Original.

Andreas Lopez fecit 1806.

Figure 20

shawl—called a *tilma*. The shawl, framed today, hangs over an altar of the basilica. It supposedly made itself in a supernatural way and shows a woman surrounded by an aureole and wearing a cloak of stars (figure 20). The entire infrastructure of all pilgrimage sites—streets, electricity, plumbing—grew simultaneously with the influx of pilgrims. But the starting point for this tremendous expense was always something supernatural. Here—and only here!—something supernatural occurred.

Was this also the case for Tikal?

There, archaeologists found small jade plates, containing fifteen Mayan symbols that have been deciphered. "The ruler of the heavenly family descended here."

With all due respect: which heavenly family? Did the ancestors of the Maya, in this geographical place—and only there!—experience something supernatural? Something so influential that the ground became a place of pilgrimage? Did the descendants of the prehistoric Maya wait for the return of some "rulers of the heavenly family"?

One of the steles of Tikal is called a "pre-classical stele," and its date of origin has been disputed. Today it is in a small museum near the ruins of Tikal. The head of the stele has been cut off, but one can recognize the chest, two bent elbows, decorated forearms, and both hands clearly have mitten-like gloves (figure 21). Below, experts recognize a horizontal crest with a double snake head. In the middle follows the spinal cord, then—still lower—a wide belt, thighs, and finally the feet. Scholars recognized a loincloth covered with jade beads and sandals on the feet. The arms seem to hold a form of a ceremonial staff, which ends in small snake heads. Hand on the heart: How objective is this observation? Wide bands lie around the wrists, and the mittens can be recognized even by a blind person (figure 22). In order to highlight the technical particulars, I have colored the image a bit (figure 23). The supposed "spinal cord" could be a bent tube that empties into a small box. A "spinal cord" must run perpendicular to the coccyx. In fact, the feet are in boots, and out of each boot winds a curious hose.

Figure 21

Figure 22

The Maya themselves were barefoot or wore sandals. What were the boots with the hoses? Was the "ruler of the heavenly family" shown here? Are bracelets, mittens, spinal cord, small boxes, boots, and hoses not just other misunderstandings of technology? Had the artist carved something in stone out of holy respect, which he himself did not understand?

The question would be absurd if it weren't for countless related representations from the world of the Maya at which to marvel. In Guatemala, not far from the Pacific coast, is the small village of El Baúl. I found the village's main attraction in an open, wind- and weather-beaten wooden shed near a sugar factory. The "El-Baúl Monument No. 27," as the stele is officially known, is 2.54 meters (8.3 ft.) tall and 1.47 meters (4.8 ft.) wide (figure 24). Decades ago it was discovered by chance in a forest clearing and left here. The stele shows a dominating figure with arms bent and hands resting on hips. The hands seem to be protected by boxing gloves, and in each hand is a tennis-ball-size ball. Thoroughly modern, the feet of the figure are in boots that reach to the knees and cover knickerbocker-like pants. A wide belt separates the pants from the close-fitting top. So far—though remarkable—this figure was dressed in the fashion of his time. But the helmet, which covers the entire head, is perplexing. Like a diving outfit, it has large coils on the shoulders (figure 25). From the helmet a tube extends to a box, similar to a tank, on the back. When observed more closely, one recognizes a spyhole in the helmet, and behind it, the nasal catheter and the left eye of the helmet wearer (figure 26).

Figure 23

Figure 24

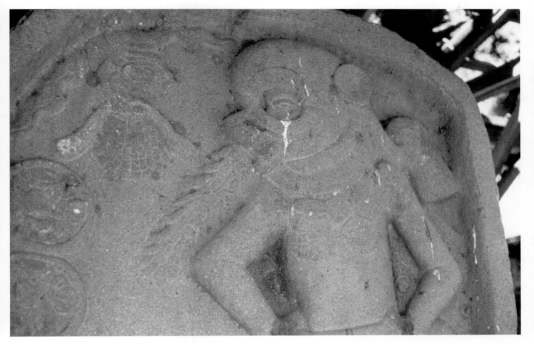

Figure 25

It gets stranger: In a direct extension of the nose, but outside of the helmet, the stonemason fashioned an animal nose, maybe that of a jaguar. Out of the snarling jaw blows—as if squeezed out—the breath of the helmet wearer. The figure wears two bands around its neck. One ends in a small square box on the chest, the other in a round something, possibly an amulet. On the foot of the stele, six goblins are sitting in the lotus position, and all are helmeted with "head horns" over the ears (figure 27). On the ground in front of the main figure lies a person with mitten-like gloves. He also has a ball that he gives to the helmet wearer.

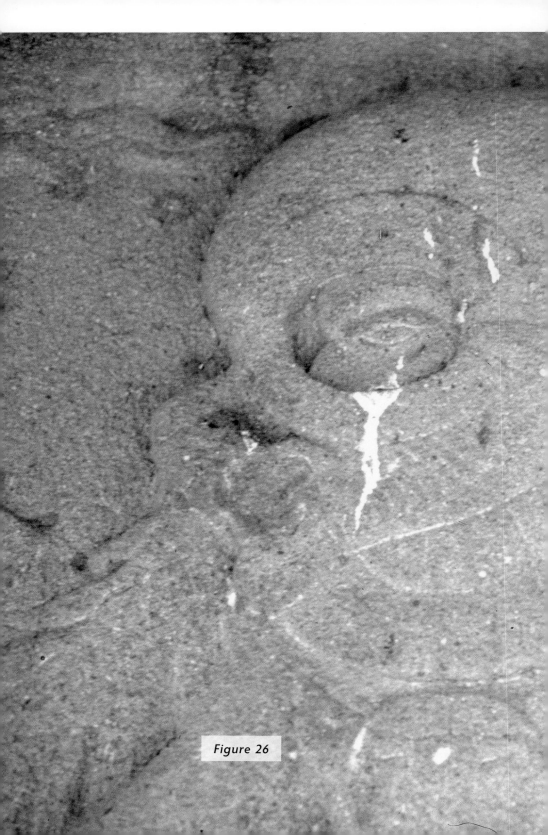

Figure 26

According to experts, the relic represents a scene from the deadly ball game of the Maya. The winner wore the mask of a monkey, jaguar, or possibly also an opossum. Therefore the "hose" from the helmet to the tank is nothing other than the tail of a small opossum, and the expressed air symbolizes water, since the opossum is a water animal.

This is an academic explanation—though ultimately as imaginative as my interpretation. Why would a ballplayer put on

Figure 27

the mask of an animal since it would only hinder him? The Maya were masters of an extremely fast game. The players had to react with lightning speed, their eyes had to see everything. The face behind the mask would have only a very limited view. And why should the player hang the tail of an opossum behind his oversized ear? What is the tank on his back? For comparison: The ballplayers of Chichén Itzá (Mexico) wore neither animal masks nor possum tails behind their ears, let alone vessels on their back.

Figure 28

I am spelling out another reading from the "cargo cult school": For a long time the predecessors of the Maya thought that "god" = extraterrestrial. He wore a closed helmet with a viewing window. This is because of the composition of the earth's air and bacteria. From one tank on the back, a chemical mixture flowed out that enriched or disinfected our air. The consumed air was expelled again. The entire body stays in a tight, air-permeable jumpsuit, finished with high boots. Just as in the example of Christian churches, the stonemason of "Monument No. 27" from El Baúl never came face to face with "god." That meeting lay far, far in the past. The detailed work of the artist originated from the fantasy of custom, similar to current artists who paint the Ascension of Jesus over a side altar, although they were not present for the actual event.

In addition, the stele from El Baúl is not the only one that shows a tank on the back. Decades ago, a strange figure came before my camera in Copán (Honduras). The stone was also worn by wind and weather over the centuries. In the end, though, a "tank" is clearly visible on the back, and on it is a type of gear wheel (figure 28). A hose goes directly from it into the helmet of the figure.

Copán is located 270 air kilometers (168 mi.) away from Tikal in present-day Honduras. In 1576, Spanish annalist Diego Garcia de Palacio had this to say about it:

> Here are the ruins of beautiful temples that demonstrate that a large city stood here, from which one cannot assume that such primitive people, assumed to be the previous residents, would have even been able to build them. . . . In between these ruins are highly remarkable things. Before you get there, you will encounter very thick walls and a giant, stone eagle. He wears a square on his chest, whose sides are of such a length that amount to a quarter of a Spanish cubit on which recognizable characters are drawn. If you step closer, you will discover the shape of a large, stone giant; the Indians said that he was the guardian of the shrine.[4]

Figure 29

Absolutely nothing remains of the "giant, stone eagle." Copán, the most important point of interest in Honduras, was named by experts the "Alexandria of the New World," Sylvanus Griswold Morley (1883–1948), the renowned American Maya researcher, maintained that Copán was the city "in which astronomy reached its highest development. It is the center of Maya science."[5]

The ruins, which were fully overgrown by the forest, were rediscovered in 1839. Approximately one hundred years later, the excavations began (figure 29). The center of Copán, with its palaces and pyramids, temples and terraces, lies higher than the wider city and is called the acropolis. Almost exactly in the middle lies the playing field with a ball court that is 26 meters long (85 ft.) and 7 meters (23 ft.) wide (figure 30). The absolute sensation is the sixty-three-step hieroglyphic stairway, which was once part of a larger temple. The list of kings is chiseled into it. Appropriately enough, all of this happened because of a ruler named Butz' Yip, a name roughly translated as "smoke is his power." On the stairs one can see carvings of sitting groups of people and some date marks. There are approximately 2,200 total Mayan glyphs—the oldest known Mayan inscriptions (figure 31). Sixteen stone priest-astronomers give advice about the complicated Mayan calendar. Here in Copán, experts discovered the digits for the beginning of this calendar, the composite number with the input glyph

Figure 30

Figure 31

"4 Ahau 8 Cumhu." It is the date on which the calendar calculation begins, which today is translated as August 14, 3114 BCE. It
is curious that at that time, there were no Maya. Either they took
over the starting point of the calendar from their predecessors, or
the Mayan culture has been around much longer than previously
thought.

The excavators and restorers did an excellent job. Copán is a
world of incomprehensible art, a visual feast for any viewer. The
pyramids are not simply made of four sloped triangular sides
pointing to heaven, for they are packed with reliefs and small figures created with the smallest details (figure 32). From the temple
walls fly down figures with aureoles (figures 33 and 34), which
elsewhere in Tulum (for example) are described as "bee gods."

Figure 32

Figure 33

Figure 34

(I will come back to that momentarily.) The inner rooms, however, are bare—at least today (figure 35).

In contrast to Tikal, Copán was built directly on the Motagua-Tal River. There was enough water here. People cut channels in monolithic blocks and sunk them into the floor. Some of these antique water pipes still function today (figures 36 to 38). We are not only components of an evolution but with our actions are subject to an evolutionary process: like technology. Originally our ancestors lived in nature, in caves, and under rock overhangs. Then they discovered the spear and the bow, and figured out how to build huts. Stonework followed, as well as construction of houses, temples, and pyramids. But behind all of it was planning. Which intellectual giant designed the phenomenal plumbing system of Copán? How many centuries was this before the "evolution of technology"?

Figure 35

Figure 36

Figure 37

Figure 38

Does Copán bear any relation to a cargo cult? Were mysterious things found in the ruin fields that would indicate a not understood ancient technology? It sounds like it. I begin with the "anthropomorphic representations," which are impressive stone blocks that often—but not always—lie in front of the pyramids. They are called anthropomorphic because the artfully carved monoliths showed mixtures of people, animals, and glyphs that hardly anyone understands (figures 39 to 41). There, into the middle of the chaos of incomprehensible artworks, dive two lower legs with shod feet (clearly visible in the middle of figure 42). Picasso had some true friends here. Then a figure crouching in the lotus position, scratching with its fingers what looks like an Asian head covering (figure 43). This could have

Figure 39

Figure 40

Figure 41

Figure 42

Figure 43

come directly from Angkor Wat in Cambodia. In addition, the excavators, in the confusion of blocks, found some with stone gears, which could not be placed anywhere (figures 44 to 46). The forest of question marks grows. Finally, irrelevant to the orthodoxy are the inexplicable spheres that turn up in many representations. We do not have the slightest idea why the stonemasons placed these spheres in their chaotic artwork. Each of the figures numbered 47 to 50 exhibits such a sphere. What did they mean? But everything ultimately has a reason for the artist. No one chiseled perverse things into the structures, probably due to the supervision of priests.

Figure 44

Figure 45

Figure 46

Figure 47

Figure 48

Figure 49

The artwork of the Maya can be readily compared with that of ancient Egyptian and ancient Indian art. In all places multicolored reliefs were created from religious thought. And in India, just as in Central America, the same steep pyramids with their ornate stuccowork can be found. What belief led to the initial spark? We basically do not experience anything different today. In the main and side altars of our cathedrals, scenes from the New and Old Testaments were represented. Archangels are accompanied by cherubs residing in the heavens. "God the Father" is enthroned between the stars and directs the grandiose events. Holy figures

Figure 50

go to heaven and are hailed as "heavenly hosts." Floating over the main altar of the Serbian cloister Dečani (Kosovo, by Peć) are two veritable UFOs with stars on their edges and a type of back beam (one is shown in figure 51, the other in figure 52). A person sits in each of these flying spheres. The one on the right looks like it is being followed by the one on the left. The Crucifixion scene together with the UFOs in the cloister of Dečani in Kosovo are from the twelfth century. What in the world inspired the painter?

The same question is valid for the entirety of religious art from antiquity, regardless of location. Understandably, people have

Figure 51

Figure 52

Figure 53

Figure 54

fabulous imaginations—but they also need inspiration. In Copán, images of priest-princes were sometimes shown with complicated stuccowork above their heads, which represents "the celestial" (figure 53). The priests themselves carried wide square beams in their hands (figure 54). One school of thought believes this represents the "scepter" of the ruler. That being said, because in this case I do not believe in the scepter variant, one question bugs me: Where does the idea of the scepter come from? Some type of powerful tool in the hands of rulers? A former weapon, cribbed from the gods? The question is not as dumb as one might think. Where does the concept of the haloes of the angels and saints come from? Why do angels clearly have wings? Because they are coming from heaven? Which heaven? The one of religious bliss or of the cosmos? Why does the bishop wear a tall hat and the pope a tiara? Why must the priests of all cultures change into especially clean clothing, before they can get closer to God? There is logic behind this seeming nonsense.

Experts are most certainly right when they argue that gods and high priests were represented there. But neither one nor the other originate from the air. These representations are definitely not of nature gods, as is often argued. They are not about the elements, thunder and lightning, earthquakes, or volcanoes. The question, which I graphically underline, is: What kind of gods? Which jewels, which ceremonial garments and modeled objects were worn by these gods and priests? Like a monkey, a person is also a great imitator, who imitates what he does not understand. Cargo cults verify that.

The helmets of the curious Mayan representations are something else. They are beautiful artistic images full of unexplained symbolism (figure 55). Above the heads are always beams of fire (figures 56 to 58). And then there are the puzzling boxes on the chest. Figures 59 and 60 demonstrate this clearly. With ten fingers, a keyboard was operated. These things must have certainly had a purpose. Did they make sounds with which one could unlock a device? Or were oscillations created, or simple control panels for a foreign technology that was copied a long time ago from some gods? Mind you, I do not believe that the Maya invented any type of computer, because that is completely wrong. Whether this scheme works for you or not, the chest boxes with keyboards are present, and they are surely used by ten fingers without gloves (figures 61 and 62). Similarly unexplained are the obviously heavy devices between the legs (figure 63). This has nothing to do with a loincloth, as someone might try to convince you.

Figure 55

Figure 56

Figure 57

Figure 58

Figure 59

Figure 60

Figure 61

Figure 62

Figure 63

I was also on the track of a misunderstood technology in the open-air storeroom of Copán. There lie the upper bodies of figures with chests where the larger operating elements must be worn (figures 64 and 65). This time there are no ten fingers on the keyboard but the fists grasp a lever on both sides, comparable to the hand-gas operation of today's machines. The hanger assembly into which the past technology had to lock is certainly there. In addition, this frame also hangs on wide bands over both shoulders. Cargo cult?

Figure 64

Figure 65

The stele in figures 66 and 67 is difficult to interpret even for experts (lower and upper part). Undoubtedly the entire body enclosed a figure of radiance. The remainder is hocus-pocus for our eyes, just like the outstanding character in figure 68. Among other things, it has a beard. The Central American Indians did not have beards.

And finally, two enlightening epiphanies for the classicists' contemplation. What served as the model for the representation of Asians in the lotus position (figure 69)? After all, we are not in a South Indian temple district but in Central America. The guy squats with crossed legs in the upper window of the stele, and even the sideways toes were not forgotten. This was, by the way, not a whim of the stonemasons. In Olmec Park in Villahermosa (Mexico), his colleagues meditate in the same manner (figures 70 and 71). Are these influences from India? How so? But there were no connections for centuries between Asia and Central America!

Figure 66

Figure 67

Figure 68

Figure 69

I have a special cargo-cult feast to offer the clever critic. What the unique artwork reveals serves as an eye-opener (figure 72). The representations on both sides of the headdress are inexplicable. But in the bottom right of the image, four fingers, the back of the hand, and the thumb are recognizable. They clearly operate a device of a technical nature. A weapon? A type of pneumatic drill? The handles of a so-called rocket belt—a one-man flying device?

I do not have an answer. But the imitation of a technical device should justifiably be in the discussion just as much as the belief in some psycho-religious ceremonial odds and ends. I can

Figure 70

Figure 71

now hear the experts saying "All wishful thinking and humbug!" Ultimately, I am familiar with the interpretations of the more honorable archaeologists. But this "humbug" resonates in many people's ears, as I will show.

In the fall of 1992, Ricardo Agurcia, the director of excavation of the Copán Project, discovered a subterranean temple. The aboveground part was named "Temple No. 16," and the subterranean part was named "Rosalia." Understandably, "Temple No. 16 is newer because it was built over "Rosalia." A spiral shaft led the excavators to a lower level, where a few isolated paintings appeared on the walls. There the men suddenly stood in front of a massive wall, painted with blue and red colors. On this wall hung the masks of gods—or human faces—and that of a supposed bird god as well as various ornaments, some of which still have not been deciphered. From that point there was a shaft that led even deeper into the cliff. Now the experts hoped to find indications of the founders of the city of Copán. Finally, even deeper, they discovered a chamber with a powerful, hermetically sealed sarcophagus. This must be it! The city father of Copán must be buried here! Chisels were wedged between the sarcophagus and the heavy lid, and the slab raised centimeter by centimeter. But the work was suddenly stopped. Mercury vapor rose out of the sarcophagus. The four working directly on the sarcophagus lid struggled for air and had to be quickly carried to the top. Mercury poisoning can be deadly. The next group could work only with gas masks. To the total amazement of the archaeologists, the sarcophagus held a sticky, mercury-containing mass. Still a bit deeper was the crypt of a woman and a sarcophagus with puzzling additions, concerning which duly competent archaeologists still remain silent today.

Three years after this discovery I spoke with the excavation leader at Copán, a highly educated Honduran who studied archaeology at Yale University. "Why is mercury in a hermetically sealed sarcophagus under a pyramid" I wanted to know. "Mercury is a color enhancer," the scholar said self-confidently. "The Maya used it to highlight the colors in their frescoes."

The simple answer, which in science is required, is nonsensical in this case. Even if mercury were used as a color enhancer, it would not be stored deep under a pyramid. Mercury has the properties of a precious metal, and it is very stable in its pure form. The silvery stuff solidifies into a crystallized mass at a temperature of −38.83° Celsius (−37.89°F). At 357° Celsius (674.6°F), it begins to boil. But it evaporates at still lower temperatures. Strangely, mercury dissolves most other metals, such as lead, copper, silver, and gold—but all at higher temperatures. Curiously, iron, silicon, nickel, and manganese cannot be dissolved. So how can mercury be stored, when it itself dissolves gold? Storage is only possible in glass, glazed stoneware (jars), or mica. Where does mercury come from? It can be released easily from ores. Steam or vinegar could be used for this process. In antiquity, quicksilver was attributed to the planet Mercury. Many peoples processed mercury. Aristotle (fourth century BCE) called it "liquid silver," and Theophrastus described mercury extraction in 315 BCE.

Figure 72

Figure 73

But the discovery of mercury at Copán is not unique. Smaller mercury discoveries were also made in Palenque and Teotihuacán (Mexico). Are mercury vapors possibly the reason for the protective helmets, masks, hoses, and boxes on the back?

But mercury discoveries were also made elsewhere. Even in the grave of Chinese emperor Qin Shi Huang (third century BCE) or in Egyptian graves on Mount Nabta, 1,350 kilometers (839 mi.) south of Cairo. There, two crypts were decorated with paintings of the goddess of heaven, Hathor. The skeletons could not be assigned to a dynasty, but in a stone jar was a crystallized mercury paste.

In ancient India, mercury (and carbide, incidentally) served as a fuel ingredient of flying machines. According to ancient Indian texts, this mercury was always transported and stored in airtight containers. These tote-boxes were made of mica.[6] So it does not surprise me that mica containers were found not only among the Maya, but also in Teotihuacán in the Mexican highlands and in North America. (I have more to say about that in my last book.[7]) Mica is not only a phenomenal electrical insulator but is also heat and acid resistant.

Anyone who also knows the temples of the Maya as well as those in south India is stunned by the parallels. Both places have brightly colored sculptures, figures sitting in the lotus position, polytheism, ornate stuccowork, and mythologies in stone. Both places also have step pyramids. The pyramids in south Indian Kanchipuram (figure 73) do not look different from those in Tikal. The tops of the Mayan pyramids are crowned with a small temple, a dwelling or landing place for the gods. On the pyramids of south India there is a Vimana, a vehicle of the gods. In both places, people have similar skin colors, faces, and gestures, and even the modern cities have developed similarly. Indian madras can be found as frequently in Mérida (Yucatán, Mexico). Without being able to verify it clearly, I sensed an obvious similarity between the holy cities of Central Americas and some in south India. Did some ancient Indians land in Central America, or was it reversed? If one follows the traditions, neither group could have sailed across the oceans, but they could have flown.

The readers of my previous books know about antique flying notions. It is clearly documented with sources.[8] In India, one of these flying groups was called the Martus. In extensive texts they were described as:

> Praise . . . which grows in the far sky or in the great expanse of the heavens. . . . Come here, Marut, from the heavens, from the air, do not stop in the distance. Your brightly flashing men in the terrible missiles, as violent as the wind, mountain shaking, Marut of thundering force. You go through the night, the days, you skilled ones, through the air, the spaces, you shakers. . . . In one day, you reach the end of the road and you stride across it the with power. . . . Where you, Marut, decide to go, you go, and fly in the heavens and on the earth.[9]

In ancient India, there were thousands of manuscripts—in Central America, too. While a large part of the ancient literature in India survived—always copied in monasteries—the Mayan manuscripts were tragically destroyed by the Spaniards. (Three manuscripts survived the chaos, but most of the writing is untranslatable.) Yet a few experts that specialize in the Parisian and Madrid codices—two of the preserved Mayan manuscripts—believe that they are about the wars between the gods in the heavens. Nothing is different in ancient Indian literature. For the majority of Mayan books a text comparison is not possible. In Indian literature no infrastructure appears for the creation of flying apparatuses—the so-called Vimanas. No workshops exist in which flying objects could be created, and there were no test flights, no evolution of technology. The flying monsters were simply there. The infrastructure came from outside: from the cosmos.

Yet the fact of the flying gods and people exists not only in India. In antiquity there was also flying in Sri Lanka, in China, or between Jerusalem and Ethiopia.[10] And the gods always came from

Figure 74

Figure 75

Figure 76

Figure 77

above. Critics believe that this is entirely normal, because where else would gods come from than the clouds? People then had only to look upward and expect salvation from above. This viewpoint is legitimate, but what is bothersome here is the omnipresent technical aftertaste. The god-priests with their keyboards on their chests, which are operated with ten fingers, with their hanger assemblies, their helmets, hoses, and boxes on their backs, their fists, clasping the technical devices—all are now present. If this strange ornamentation can be found in only one place, I would not say a word about it. There is also the phenomenon of the not-understood ceremonies that migrated into the religions and sculptures. And the baffling head assemblies leave open questions that have never been satisfactorily answered by archaeology. Maybe because the cargo element was not taken into account. And prehistoric aviation is something like a mortal sin in the school of archaeology. Sacrilege.

What did the ancient Indian texts say that honored the divine Maruts? "Praise . . . which grows in the far sky or in the great expanse of the heavens. . . . Come here, Marut, from the heavens, from the air, do not stop in the distance. Your brightly flashing men . . ." Figures 66 and 67 (pages 66–67) do not show anything different; both are arranged so their bodies are fully surrounded by rays.

Tulum is on the Caribbean coast of Mexico. It was a city built according to a plan. The main streets run parallel to the north-south direction, and the temple is raised on multiple levels similar to the white lighthouses on the green-blue Caribbean Sea (figures 74 to 76, pages 77–79).

Today, Tulum is a truly dreary place of ruins, which is located slightly off the tourist route. The temples of Tulum were, according to the prevailing view, sacred to the bee god. Artistic sculptural representations show anything but an industrious honey collector, mainly figures with thoroughly human faces flying down from the sky. Their legs are always pointing upward and the helmeted head, if it has not been cut off, points toward the earth (figures 77 to 81).

Figure 78

Figure 79

Figure 80

The relief in the main temple of Tulum is difficult to recognize. Yet the spread legs can be seen, and the shoes seem to be on something like bearings. The arms are angled, and I would love to press joysticks into the fists (figures 82 and 83). Even the wings are stylized right and left, and the jumpsuit with the helmet make for a perfect god descending from the heavens.

Figure 81

Figure 82

Figure 83

Figure 84

Figure 85

A bee? I think we have forgotten to see what there is to see. In the stucco representations of Tulum, I see misunderstood technologies. Presumably no stonemason observed any type of being that comes headfirst out of the clouds. But the religious tradition taught them that once a humanlike being with mysterious gadgets came from above. These mysterious teachers have promised to return, and people anxiously awaited the arrival of any all-powerful gods from the past. The motif of headfirst, down-moving gods was not confined to Tulum. They also exist in other Mayan locations. Here are some examples from Chichén Itzá (figures 84 to 87).

Figure 86

Figure 87

Figure 88

In Olmec Park in La Venta—which lies in Villahermosa, Mexico—stand powerful, plump heads with tightly fitting helmets (figure 88). They were found a few kilometers apart in the marsh of the surrounding area. Gods? Priests? Warriors? We do not know. The so-called dragon monolith can be admired in the same park. Here, in a closed chamber, sits a human form with its helmet—the dragon. In its right hand it carries a rod, and a square box hangs over its head (figure 89). Did people want to represent the flying monster with the fire-breathing dragon?

And finally there is Stele No. 3. It measures 4.27 meters (14 ft.) by 2.03 meters (6.66 ft.). Unfortunately many parts of the artistic representation have crumbled. After all, one recognizes on the upper right part a figure with a helmet floating above. The figure points downward in an instructive gesture, and its legs are directed upward (figures 90 and 91).

Figure 89

Figure 90

Things are not much different in our churches when we place the angels between the heavens and the earth.

My pictures from the world of the Maya should serve as food for thought and lead to new questions. Indeed, archaeology collects and arranges facts, but with regard to the imaginative world of the artists who created their splendid sculptures, the archaeology I admire also falls into its own trap of established patterns of thought. The "heavenly" is not only a starry canopy, the expression "heaven" is not only a place wished for after death. Heaven is also outer space. And there are various old texts describing people who are brought "into the heavens" and are astoundingly brought back to earth intact, which shows that "heaven" can be a misunderstood description of "the mother ship in orbit." Such a visit "to heaven" (in the mother ship) was described for millennia by different people, among them figures such as Enoch and Abraham.[11] And all

Figure 91

this before the big flood. People have marveled at the firmament since Adam's time, and not only because it is silent, mysterious, and infinite but also because unexplainable objects moved there and visited the earth with "smoke and fire" (figure 92). This is described in the text of the divine Maruts: "which grows in the far sky or in the great expanse of the heavens . . . Come here, Marut, from the heavens, from the air, do not stop in the distance . . . and fly in the heavens and on the earth."

It is clear that "heaven" was never meant to be a place of bliss after death. "Heaven" was "outer space." This is valid for countless old texts from Indian Sanskrit schools, for Solomon's air cars in the Ethiopian Kebra Nagast, for the book of Enoch, the "Abraham Apocrypha," and the Old Testament:[12]

> It rained down brimstone and fire on Sodom and Gomorrah from the Lord of the heavens. . . . (Genesis 19:24)

> It came to pass in the thirtieth year, on the fifth day of the fourth month . . . the heavens opened up. . . . I saw something come like a whirlwind from the north and a large cloud surrounded from beaming grace and an incessant fire . . . and their legs were straight and glistened like ore. . . . I further saw a wheel on the ground . . . and the four wheels were of the same shape. (Ezekiel 1:1ff.)

Any citation will attest: "heaven" actually meant outer space. The same determination is also valid for some Pyramid Texts of ancient Egypt[13] or for the "legend of the winged solar discs." "Thereafter, the hat of Hor flies toward the sun in a shape of a large sun disc with wings . . . as he saw enemies from the heavenly height . . . he stormed them so violently that they neither saw nor heard him."[14]

And what does all of this have to do with Central America? The heavenly beings of the Maya and their ancestors were the same extraterrestrial astronauts as elsewhere. And they left their traces not only in misunderstood technologies, in unidentifiable attributes of godly statues—but also in monumental structures.

Figure 92

Figure 93

Figure 94

Places to
Honor the Gods

Approximately 40 kilometers (25 mi.) northeast of Mexico City lie the grandiose ruins of Teotihuacán (figure 93). In July of 1520, Hernando Cortes, the conqueror of Mexico, rode past and did not notice the massive installations concealed under the hills. The Aztecs always knew, but they did not speak about it. The word *Teotihuacán* stems from this location and means "the place where one becomes God." The conscientious Franciscan missionary Bernardino de Sahagún (1499–1590) noted: "They named the place Teotihuacán, because it was the burial place of the gods."[1]

Presumably the old Indians were right. By means of ground-penetrating radar in the summer of 2009 a tunnel was in fact located under the ruins of Teotihuacán at a depth of 12 meters (39 ft.). As in the ancient pyramids of Giza (Egypt) high-tech robots were also recently used in Mexico (figure 94). A four-wheeled machine with the name Tlaloque I left tracks of 124 meters (407 ft.) and discovered three chambers that were blocked with tons of heavy monoliths. Something immense lies under the buried area. Teotihuacán was a holy place, a pilgrimage site for honoring the gods. Bernardino de Sahagún noted: "During the night-time, as the sun does not shine, it is said that the gods gathered and advised them at this place, which was named Teotihuacán."[2]

These divine gatherings included Citlalicue, goddess of the starry sky, and the red Tezcatlipoca, the god with starry robes. According to another tradition,[3] Quetzalcoatl/Kukumatz, the god of the moon and the morning star, was also present during the deliberations. Tensions and hope are running high regarding the discovery of an explosive finding in the subterranean chambers. Finally, no one would enclose three rooms under the earth with massive stones—if they were empty or contained unimportant objects.

It is unknown who built Teotihuacán. Laurette Séjourné, who was the archaeologist leading the excavations of Teotihuacán for years, noted:

Figure 95

The origins of this high culture represent the most inaccessible of secrets. . . . If it is difficult to accept that cultural characteristics were found in the beginning of their definitive imprint, so it is more difficult to conceive that the corresponding complex spiritual conditions—fully formed—suddenly simply existed. We do not have any material evidence for this astounding process of development.[4]

What Ms. Séjourné missed is the evolution of technology. According to the prevailing view, Teotihuacán was built somewhere between 500 BCE and 650 CE. That is a long time period, but in every generation, the architects and builders must have

Figure 96

Figure 97

kept ancient plans. (I personally maintain that the origins of Teotihuacán are much older.) Such an architectural constraint can only be understood by the influence of a powerful, all-controlling religion.

With its large surface area and its perfect infrastructure, Teotihuacán is still a place of wonder today. From north to south, Grand Street, called Camino de los Muertos (Street of the Dead) is 40 meters (131 ft.) wide and three kilometers (1.86 mi.) long. It is flanked on both sides with smaller pyramidal platforms. In the northern direction the boulevard has a slope of 30 meters (98.4 ft.), and an optical illusion is created, one for which every visitor still falls. From the south—that is, from below—the tourist sees endless evenly sized steps that finally merge with the moon pyramid at the end of the avenue (figure 95, pages 100–101). Conversely, when observed from the other direction, all steps—abracadabra!—disappear, and observers see only the 3 kilometers of the Street of the Dead in front of them (figure 96).

Viewed from the moon pyramid, to the left is the largest monumental structure of Mesoamerica—the sun pyramid (figures 97 and 98). It has a square base of 222 meters (728 ft.)

by 225 meters (738 ft.) and is 19 meters (62 ft.) taller than the moon pyramid at the end of the boulevard. Nevertheless, the observer on the pyramid top forms an impression that both structures are the same height on the basis of the slope in the Street of the Dead. Incidentally, the sun pyramid is even of more massive proportions than the Pyramid of Cheops in Giza. In Egypt, the pyramids were built with monoliths, heavy stone blocks; in Teotihuacán, they were built with smaller stones and millions of air-dried clay bricks. As paint residues demonstrate,

Figure 98

the pyramids were previously painted in loud colors. Today, gigantic figures, which once stood there, are missing from the flattened pyramids. A 3-meter (9.8 ft.) tall, 22,000-kilogram (48,502 lb.) heavy statue once lay at the foot of the moon pyramid, and a silver and gold-plated deity stood at the sun pyramid. It still existed during the time of the Spanish conquerors, but the first bishop of Mexico, the Franciscan Juan de Zumárraga (1468–1548), allowed them to be ground up and melted down.[5]

The third-largest structure of Teotihuacán is the citadel with the

Quetzalcoatl temple. Where—by the way—all these name choices are absurd. They did not stem from the builders. Quetzalcoatl was the flying god of the Aztecs and Maya, and the "citadel" has as little to do with a fortification as a Hindu temple with Zurich's central railway station. And the names moon pyramid, sun pyramid, Street of the Dead, and so on, are all inventions of our world. After all, the so-called Quetzalcoatl temple is the most beautiful and richest stucco-decorated structure of Teotihuacán. Feather-adorned snake heads wind through the peripheral frieze, and masks of demonic beings gawk from the slopes of the stone walls (figures 99 and 100). The motifs of the Quetzalcoatl temple confirm that the emblem of the winged snake god was known to the Aztecs and Maya for a long period of time. The representations are almost identical to the later representations of the god Quetzalcoatl of the Aztecs or Kukulkan/Kukumatz of the Maya. Paintings were found in the interior of some structures of Teotihuacán that no one is quite clever enough to interpret. Indeed, there was talk about a jaguar or puma god, but what he spews or eats is not identifiable (figure 101), just like the flying heads with their confusing head constructions (figure 102).

Figure 99

Figure 100

Figure 101

Meanwhile, Teotihuacán has been proven to be a grandiose model of our solar system. This was discovered by U.S. engineer Hugh Harleston Jr., who worked at Teotihuacán for years.[6] Being an engineer, Harleston thought that each plan had a unifying measure, and in the structures of Teotihuacán overall, he found a measurement unit of 57 meters (187 ft.) or a multiple thereof, or that buildings stood in distances from each other that were divisible by 57. Along the Camino de los Muertos all structures are separated by 114 (2 × 57) or 342 (6 × 57) meters. The wall of the citadel measures exactly 399 (7 × 57) meters.

Harleston was searching for a smaller measure: he divided 57 by 3. The result—19—spoke to more structures whose side lengths were exactly 19 meters. Given his profession, he thought there would be smaller measures, and he sought to find the smallest measurement that was associated with all Teotihuacán structures. He found it with 1.059 meters. He called this measure *hunab*—a Mayan word that means something similar to unity. All measured data have series of multiple *hunabs*.

The Quetzalcoatl pyramid and the sun and moon pyramids are, respectively, 21, 42, and 63 *hunab* tall. Their heights are in relation to one another as 1 : 2 : 3. Computer analysis found something astounding: the ground plan of the Quetzalcoatl pyramid corresponds to the millionth part of the pole radius (= circumference of the earth at the Arctic Circle). Harleston also discovered at the citadel multiple Pythagorean triangles, the number pi, as well as the number 299,792, which is known to us from the speed of light (229,792 km/h).

The pyramid frustums and the platforms of the citadel stood for the average orbital periods of planets Mercury, Venus, Earth, and Mars. Directly behind the citadel flows the San Juan River in a man-made canal dug by the original builders. This canal lies in the place exactly where the asteroid belt lies between Mars and Jupiter in our solar system. A creek with many stones symbolized the asteroid belt with its hundreds of thousands of protruding rocks. Piece by piece the buildings on the Street of the Dead are a model of our

Figure 102

Figure 103

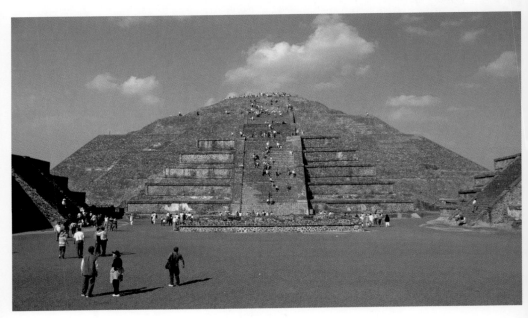

Figure 104

solar system (figure 103). In the extended line behind the moon pyramid (figure 104) is a hill. There Harleston found the ruins of smaller temples that earlier stood for the outer planets Neptune and Pluto. All distances are correct, precisely measured in *hunabs*.

Thus it becomes astronomical. At the time of the creation of Teotihuacán, regardless if this happened two or four thousand years ago, the builders could not have known anything about the asteroid belt between Mars and Jupiter. Even the planets Uranus, Neptune, and Pluto were unknown at the time. Uranus was first discovered in 1781. Neptune was added to the list of planets in 1846, and Pluto just joined in 1930. Recently, the International Astronomical Union (IAU) agreed to change the planetary status of Pluto. With its 6,000 kilometer (3,728 mi.) circumference, the astronomers argued that it is too small to be a planet. This does not change anything because Pluto has been in orbit around the sun for millennia. It does not matter if it is classified as a planet or dwarf planet.

Understandably, people did the dirty work of Teotihuacán. There were people who dried clay bricks, transported stones, and piled them on top of one another. People dug tunnels and mixed colorful chemicals. But the directors behind it all came from elsewhere. Everywhere in the past people were able to accomplish formidable architectural feats. Why? Where is the incentive, the enthusiasm? The answer is always: for the gods. To honor the gods, to find favor with the gods, to be liked and not punished by the gods. We therefore have phenomenal ceremonial sites across the globe. These gods were not forces of nature, were neither sun, nor moon, nor volcanic eruptions. Why not? Because the gods spoke, because they had precise instructions and many people were instructed, as recorded in countless traditions. The gods never dirtied their hands. They never engaged in the practical and difficult work (apart from the creation of smaller basecamps for themselves).

In Teotihuacán—and elsewhere in Maya Land—the birth of the gods is demonstrated every day. On the large area of the citadel is an approximately 30-meter (98.4 ft.) tall wooden pole, anchored firmly in the ground. Four Indians in painted shirts and

Figure 105

colorful hats stand in front of it and place small flutes to their lips. Sometimes with lowered, sometimes with heaven-turned heads, they dance around the pole. One of them beats a small hand drum. Then each of them climbs the mast, pulling a rope behind him. At the very top the rope is tied around the right ankle. On an agreed signal, all four men tilt backward from the mast and fall below. The rope prevents an abrupt fall, and the men turn in wide circles around the pole. Their arms are spread apart like wings (figures 105 to 109). The length of the rope is calculated so that each man circles the pole exactly thirteen times before he then touches the earth with his hands. All of this has a meaning

Figure 106

Figure 107

Figure 108

in the Mayan calendar. There are four men with thirteen turns, so 4 × 13 = 52. Two-hundred and fifty years are in a calendar cycle. The Maya believed that every fifty-two years—or multiples thereof—the gods of the stars would come back to earth.

These fliers are named Los Voladores, and the show is nothing other than mythology in practice, performed for centuries to the present day. How was that with the so-called bee gods of Tulum? They were also headfirst, chiseled in stone.

Astronomers and mathematicians practice an exact science. For them, every number must be correct and confirmable. In his book *Teufelswerk* (*Devil's Work*), mathematician Paul H. Krannich proves a clear connection between the Great Pyramids of Giza and Teotihuacán.[7] Put the same teachers behind both places. There is—mathematically—no way around it.

Figure 109

Independently from this, astronomer Dr. Wolfgang Feix also found a mathematical connection between both locations.[8] Additionally, Feix postulated that the sun pyramid of Teotihuacán contained a message referring to Alpha Centauri, the star lying closest to Earth. Earlier, experts believed that no planets revolved around Alpha and Proxima Centauri. However, people see that differently now. Calculations based on data from NASA's Kepler telescope suggest there are at least fifty billion planets in our galaxy alone. One percent of these—and this is the absolute lowest value!—orbit in zones around their sun that are neither too hot nor too cold. Fifty billion planets are in the so-called ecosphere, the living zone. How much do you want to bet that these numbers quickly rise? And do you want to bet that the subterranean crypts of Teotihuacán turn up something extraordinary? As long as we ordinary citizens are not denied access as we were regarding the alleged cult objects in the sarcophagus under the Temple No. 16 from Copán. Or the rooms under the pyramid on the plateau of Giza. As elsewhere, there are some very serious people in archaeology, skeptics as well, who consider themselves to be highly responsible. Others may not know what they know. But in electronically connected times, in a world of shorter distances, secrecy leads to foolishness. It damages precisely the guild to which they belong: archaeology.

Not only in Teotihuacán is there a stone monument for the gods—the same is true in today's tourist metropolis Chichén Itzá in Yucatán. Earlier, experts differentiated between a "new" and "old" realm of the Maya. The Chichén Itzá of the tourists is considered a "new" realm, first established around 800 CE. The old Chichén Itzá, named Chichén Viejo, gets almost no visitors (figures 110 and 111). The origins of the old Chichén Itzá are a mystery. When a church falls to ruin today a new one is built. In this process the Christian symbols still remain, and they outlast the decay of the old building. The same happened in Chichén Itzá. The main god of Chichén Itzá was Kukulkan or Kukumatz (Quetzalcoatl to the Aztecs). The same figure is

Figure 110

Figure 111

always meant, and this Kukulkan, according to tradition, comes from a distant land or, for the Maya, from the Morning Star. In Chichén Itzá, the winged snake, or the heavenly being crowned with rays of light, is ubiquitous (figures 112 and 113). According to old tales, the face of this god Kukulkan was hidden behind a mask. He supposedly wore a strange hat and was bejeweled with glowing necklaces and ankle bracelets. The Mesoamerican people passed down that they learned the science of mathematics and astronomy from him, and that he also taught arts and crafts and issued laws.[9] His birth was described as supernatural and, after completing his "developmental aid," he was pulled up

Figure 112

Figure 113

"on the shores of the heavenly waters"[10] and was immolated of his own free will. So in the imaginative world of the Maya he was associated with the Morning Star. Another version declares that he was carried away to the heavens, and a third will even tell of Kukulkan climbing onto a magical raft of snakes and return-ing to his homeland. But all traditions have in common that Kukulkan promised to return at a much later time.

But the most original, "real" Kukulkan, was a "heaven snake," a "heavenly monster," who "came to earth in intervals."[11] This unrivaled Kukulkan was closely connected from the beginning with Itzamna, the highest heavenly god of the Maya. He was the lord of the heavens enthroned in the clouds. Represented as an old man, his body was decorated with planetary symbols and astro-nomical signs, and—contradictions or not—he was at the same time a kind of two-headed dragon.

To honor Kukulkan, astronomy bloomed in the entire realm of the Maya. The observatory at Chichén Itzá at first glance looks like a modern observatory (figure 114). Sitting on three terraces, the rotunda rises over the jungle. Inside, winding stairs lead to the highest lookout. There are hatches and openings that are oriented to specific Mayan star constellations. The Maya were deeply concerned with Mars, Jupiter, Saturn, and the Pole Star, as well as constellations such as Orion, Gemini, and the Pleiades. They knew that earth's orbit around the sun was 365.2421 days. They were also familiar with the relationships between different planets. When Mars is at point X, where is Venus in relation to Jupiter? The Maya knew this. They calculated the orbit of Venus around the sun so precisely that they were off by only one day in a time span of 6,000 years.[12] But the Maya did not exist for 6,000 years. They must have obtained their information from an older culture or from some heavenly teacher. The Maya even had a table of eclipses for their geographical area from which all possible eclipses, whether past or future, could be read.

The inconceivable dates of Mayan astronomy shocked Professor Robert Henseling sixty years ago. Henseling studied Mayan astronomy for years and came to the following conclusion:

It cannot be questioned that the Mayan astronomers' star constellations, which go back for millennia, can be reliably

Figure 114

traced back to a specific type and day. . . . This would be incomprehensible if not in past history, that is, thousands of years before the beginning of Christian time reckoning, the corresponding observations *had been made by someone somewhere and reliably handed down to future generations. . . .* [And further:] Such an achievement importantly presupposes *that since prehistory, a development of a very long duration took place* (emphasis added).[13]

Or the other way around: The so-called gods trained some clever Mayan lads in astronomy.

But even during and after the Spanish conquest the Chilam Balam books were written in Central America. *Chilam* means "prophet" or "translator for the gods," and *balam* means "jaguar."

These books differ from one another by the respective discovery location being added to the name. So there is a Chilam Balam book from Mani, one from Balam, another from Chumayel, from Ixil, from Tekax, and so on. The books, in Latin letters, but written in Yucatecan, were created between the sixteenth and eighteenth centuries. The contents were collected by many priests and transcribed by many hands. The entirety is a mixture of ancient stories and obscure prophecies—making for an often difficult read. The sources, however, from which the priests obtained their information were ancient. These original sources are missing simply because the Spanish destroyed all Mayan writings (except for three, two of which are almost impossible to decipher). One might ask how that almost five-hundred-year-old book could say anything about the origin of humanity and the gods. Yet, I know Muslims, for example, who can recite the Qur'an word for word. I've met Christians who have the entire New Testament memorized, and Jews who on the spot recalled the Torah—the Pentateuch with the five books of Moses—from memory. Even when they do not know it word for word, many devotees know the essential content of their religion. If in a terrible war all Bibles were reduced to ashes, some priests and religious laypeople who survived could resurrect the holy scriptures and write them down again. The same happened in Central America in the sixteenth century. Priests and tribal elders collected memories and traditions from the time of the gods. Only the paper on which everything was written was new. The creation of the earth reads in the Chilam Balam book of Chumayel as follows:

> This is the history of the world in those times, because it has been written down, because the time has not yet ended for

making these books . . . so that Maya men may be asked if they know how they were born here in this country. . . .

It was Katun 11 Ahau [date], when Ah Mucencah [god traveling down] came forth. . . . Then it was that fire descended, then the rope descended, then rocks and trees descended.[14]

In the Chilam Balam book from Mani, the descent of each of the gods was explained: "This is the report of the descent of a god, the thirteen gods, and a thousand gods, as the priests of Chilam Balam, Xupan, Nauat . . . instructed."[15]

In addition to these Chilam Balam books in Central America, there also exist old Mexican manuscripts of motley texts with many images, found by the smart abbé Charles-Étienne Brasseur de Bourbourg. This abbé had a genius for languages. In Mexico he learned Aztec, and with the help of Aztec priests he could decode the ancient manuscripts. One of these manuscripts gave Brasseur the name of his Indian teacher: Chimalpopoca. The text is therefore known as Codex Chimalpopoca.[16] According to this codex, the gods first created the heaven and the earth, then fire rained down. Afterward, the gods discussed which of them would live on earth in the future: "Grief-stricken, they considered the deity with the starry robe, of the starry realms, the mistress in the water, who comes over the people and stomps the earth, Quetzalcoatl."

In the same codex it was also claimed that the sun shone first in the fifth century, and in this world age "was grounded the earth, heaven, and the four kinds of human inhabitants." It remains incomprehensible how ancient Mexicans knew about the four kinds of human inhabitants.

Positively dramatic is the account of a spooky world inferno that is described as an eerie night of darkened sun: "The second sun was created. Four jaguars were its symbols of days. It is called the jaguar sun. It is suitable that the heaven collapsed and the sun at that time did not follow its path. At noon it was directly overhead, and night immediately followed."

What is this about? A shift? An abrupt shift of the earth's axis? An inexplicable spectacle in the age of the third sun would lead to an absolute global catastrophe: "It is called fire-rain sun. In this age, it occurred that fire rained and the people burned. . . . The elders explained that in those days, the stony sands that we see today were strewn about and they foamed in bubbly andesitic lava, and then were stored in different reddish rocks."

An unnatural gap exists between Mars and Jupiter where thousands of asteroids tumble about. Even today, the origin of this asteroid belt is controversial. One theory holds that the debris comes from an exploded planet. The description in the Codex Chimalpopoca goes superbly well with this theory. The explosion of a planet in our solar system would eclipse our sun for months or even years. Cosmic dust would be drawn through the solar system, glowing debris would strike the earth. White-glowing bombs would shred the thin, delicate skin of our planet, and it would shake and rattle—not only from the cosmic projectiles but also from the displacement of the gravitational forces of the solar system. The exploded planet knocked the complex structure of the orbits of our planets out of balance. Floods, a darkened sun, and rain of fire were the logical consequences. It must have appeared to the inhabitants of earth that the sky was burning and falling down upon them. All the elements would be raging: the oceans pouring over landmasses, hurricanes lashing bodies of water, and volcanoes erupting everywhere.

Is this what was described in Codex Chimalpopoca? The continuation of the drama was described in the Popol Vuh, the holy book of the Quiché Maya. One can read there how people wandered aimlessly and struggled to find shelter from the raging violence. Close to starvation, more and more Indians arrived at the top of Mount Hacavitz—which was also called the resting place. They stood freezing in the endless night, huddled around the images of the gods, not understanding what was happening:

> There is no sleep for you, no peace. The lamentations in the innermost part of your hearts are large, that the day will not dawn, that it will not be light. Only despondency is in your expressions, sadness and dejection came over you, and you are bewildered by anguish. . . . Oh, if we could only see the sun be born, you said and spoke with one another. . . . Then the sun came out. And small and large animals rejoiced, all standing on the rivers and in canyons; and those who were on the peaks of the mountains looked together to where the sun emerged.[17]

Generously calculated, the Mayan empire lasted from 1500 BCE to 1600 CE. In this time span, however, there were no global catastrophes. The Egyptians, Babylonians, Greeks, and also Romans have reported nothing about that. In the past 3,000 years, the sun was not darkened, and the sky has not burned, no flood has destroyed the surface of the earth, and no "gods" descended from the heavens. And so one must assume that the events described in the chronicles of the Central American Indians occurred before the time of their own existence.

Here there is a cross-reference in Greece. There, around 400 BCE, the philosophers Plato, Socrates, and others gathered. Their conversations were meticulously transcribed by students who sat behind them. In the dialogue titled *Critias,* which is about Atlantis, Plato insists that the Egyptians would have preserved all the records from ancient times in written documents deposited in the temples prior to the disaster.[18] After recording these temple documents, a war broke out between Atlantis and the mainland, which occurred 9,000 years ago. If one calculates from the time of Plato to then, that is approximately 11,400 years ago. This is odd, because the Greek historian Herodotus, called the father of history, also commented about a similar time period. In the second book of his *Histories,* Herodotus wrote about his visit to Thebes, which is present-day Luxor. The priests showed him 341 statues and gave a brief commentary on each one. These 341 statues corresponded to 11,340 years. Before these 11,340 years, the gods were on the earth: "Since these 11,340 years, there were no more gods who mingled with humans in Egypt. . . . And the Egyptians certainly would know this, because they have consistently calculated and described the years of the kings and high priests."[19]

Why are there no written records from that time that go back 10,000 years? Look up Plato:

The reason for this is as follows: There have been, and will be again, many destructions of mankind arising out of many causes; the greatest have been brought about through the agencies of fire and water, and other lesser ones, by innumerable other causes. There is a story, which even you have preserved, that once upon a time, Phaëton, the son of Helios, having yoked the steeds in his father's chariot, because he was not able to drive them in the path of his father, burnt up all that was upon the earth, and was himself destroyed by a thunderbolt. Now this has the form of a myth, *but really signifies a*

*declination of the bodies moving in the heavens around the earth,
and a great conflagration of things upon the earth, which recurs
after long intervals. . .* (emphasis added).[20]

If Plato is correct, *x* number of centuries ago a planetary catastrophe must have occurred in our solar system: *"a declination of the
bodies moving in the heavens around the earth."* How would anyone
know about planetary orbits 2,400 years ago? In the seventeenth
century, Galileo Galilei was to be killed because of his planetary
message. The Inquisition wanted that. But everything that Galileo
preached could already be gleaned from Plato. Moreover, a planetary catastrophe would have also affected other people on the
planet. Finally, the earth is a sphere that rotates once around its
axis every twenty-four hours.

Plato in ancient Greece does not say anything fundamentally
different from what was handed down by the Maya. There as well
were accounts of a world conflagration, of a sun that disappeared, of
terrible natural catastrophes, all of which were caused by the devia-
tion of the heavenly bodies orbiting the sun. The Maya provided
some dramatic particulars to the same events that Plato spoke of.

For the Maya, even in their new world astronomy served as
the most admirable of all the sciences. They were downright
obsessed with it. With it all heavenly observations fell into two
main categories: first, changes and movements in the firmament, and second, cosmic catastrophes. This was validated by
the Franciscan missionary and cultural researcher Bernardino
de Sahagún (1500–1590). He not only researched the language
of the Aztecs but also that of the Nahua. This group of Indian
tribes already existed at the time of the Toltecs—approximately
100 BCE. Their language, Nahuatl, was spoken at the time
of Bernardino de Sahagún primarily by the rural population.

Bernardino de Sahagún was the head of the College of Santa Cruz on the Caribbean coast. Countless Indians went there on and off; Sahagún would sit together with them for weeks, nurturing friendships and asking them to report to him what they knew about the history of their tribes. So arose a transcript of records, the *Historia general de las cosas de la Nueva España* (*General History of Things in New Spain*). There, the Indians described their fears regarding phenomena in the sky:

> At nightfall, people were very scared, hoping, as was said, that luckily the fire driller would not fall. Then people would perish, people would be at the end, and it would last all night. The sun would not rise again so that it would be completely dark. Then would the Tzitzitzimi monster come down and destroy the people . . . and no one fell down on the ground, so they said, but people climbed on their rooftops. And so every person suspected, that he should take heed of the stars, whose names are the Many and the Fire Driller.[21]

In the *Historia general,* "smoking stars" were also mentioned, but it is not clear if this meant meteors or shooting stars. And as the sun disappeared, even some gods observed the disturbed heavens: "As they say, there were those who watched there: Quetzalcoatl, whose nickname is Ecatl; also Totec, or the lord of the ring; the red Tezcatlipoca; and those that are called serpents of the clouds."[22]

The same Franciscan monk, Bernardino de Sahagún, also described a ball game played by the Mayans as well as the Aztecs in the highlands and that was originally brought to earth by the gods. The Aztecs called this game *tlachtli,* and an Aztec team demonstrated their *tlachtli* in a Spanish courtyard. It happened like this:

After Hernando Cortez (1485–1547) conquered Central America, he came home under fire. Emperor Charles V (1500–1558) ordered him to a hearing in a Spanish court. In addition to the precious loot, the clever Cortez brought an Aztec ball team to Spain and had them play before high society. The game was played on a rectangular court of 40 by 15 meters (approximately 131 by 49 feet) that was bordered by a wall. Above, on the parapets, sat the royal lords with their entourage. Spoiled by many daily attractions of diverse kinds, many had become settled in their boredom. But soon the conversation of the men in their plush trousers and ruffs was silenced, and the women waved their ivory-jeweled fans more quickly. What happened on the playing field below was breathtaking. Nothing comparable had yet been seen in the Old World.

Thoroughly fit, the loincloth-dressed Aztecs played with a five-pound, elastic ball made out of a strange material, which they called rubber. The match had strict rules: The heavy, black ball could not be touched with the hands or feet and it could not touch the ground. The ball was kept in play through quick-reacting bodily movements from the hips, shoulders, elbows, thighs, or knees. In a headlong dive, the Indians threw themselves at the ball, hitting it with any body part other than hands and feet to a fellow player, who tried to pass the hard rubber ball through a stone ring set in the wall in the middle of the playing field. As much as possible, the opponent should never have possession of the ball, otherwise he would try, for his part, to knock the ball through the ring. A murderous game, in which nasal bones shattered, bones broke, and players heading the ball were knocked unconscious. "Many players were carried away dead," reported a witness, "or they sustained heavy injuries on their bodies."[23]

This ball game that the Aztecs performed was a thousand years old. The Aztecs adopted it from the Maya, and they in turn

Figure 115

had learned it from the gods. That is also what the bishop Diego de Landa—the same one that allowed Mayan manuscripts to be destroyed while at the same time compiling a book about the Maya—originally reported: the gods were the players.[24]

It is no surprise that every large Maya city was equipped with a ball field. In Chichén Itzá, there still exist some of the old—and today partially restored—reliefs on the right and left side of the playing field. And no one can figure them out. Figures 115 and 116 show a priest—if it even is one(!)—with a feather headdress on his head, a tube in his nose, and ear protection. The figure is placed in a pompous, apparently padded jumpsuit, closed with a belt buckle, out of which a "scepter" protrudes. The knee protection and thickly soled shoes complete the image. But what is the figure holding in his hands? Four fingers are around a handle, secured to a rectangular object. The object seems to symbolize danger, as the animal snout with the canine tooth indicates. There are many of these guys. The man behind him holds a similar article, this time angled in the direction of the ground. Slightly modified objects are carried by other "priests" (figure 117). Cargo cult? Some technology copied from the gods? We smart-alecks so far have come up with nothing meaningful regarding the technological-looking objects. Containers for blood or snake heads are vaguely discussed. A tour guide, whom I listened to while he led a French group through the ball field, surpassed everyone. To the question from a woman regarding what the objects in their hands were, he said: "Those are irons!" Quite simple, right?

All people worshipped gods, but the opinions about these gods could not be more controversial. In Maya Land the heavenly figures clearly stemmed from traditions. They are understood as real, corporeal figures. And in Chichén Itzá the priests and architects brought it to completion, and their descending gods were immortalized in a structure that still stands today: the Kukulkan

Figure 116

Figure 117

pyramid (figure 118). It is 30 meters (98.4 ft.) tall, placed on a square base with a 55.5 meter (182 ft.) side length. The structure consists of nine platforms lying one above the other, which are bisected in the middle with wide staircases. Each of these four staircases has 91 steps plus the topmost platform. Each step stands for a day. This results in $4 \times 91 = 364$, plus the highest platform equals 365—the number of days in a year. Each pyramid side is organized in 52 artistically decorated stone panels. Fifty-two years make up the smallest Mayan calendar cycle (figures 119 and 120). While the Egyptian pyramids are set up in a north-south and east-west direction, the north-south axis goes diagonally through the Chichén Itzá structure (figure 121). That was the intent. The astronomical orientation, but also the angle of inclination of the pyramids and the nine stacked platforms, result in a grandiose spectacle year after year.

At sunrise on December 21 the first rays of the sun shine on the eastern half of the pyramid (figure 122). While it gradually climbs higher on the horizon, on the pyramid's northern surface and

Figure 118

Figure 119

indeed exactly on the edges of the steps, a band of light and shadows can be seen. The effect results from the nine terraces, the angle of inclination, and the astronomical orientation (figure 123). Then the light and shadow band creeps slowly down the steps and is united at the bottom of the stairs with the head of Kukulkan. Not content with that, on June 21 the spectacle repeats on the other side of the pyramid, but in the opposite way. At sunset the sun first shines on the head of Kukulkan at the lower edge of the stairs. The lower the sun sinks, the darker waves defined by sunlight creep slowly up the steps (figure 124). During sunset the small temple on the pyramid top is lit up in a bizarre light show. As the sun disappears behind the horizon the specter disappears.

Figure 120

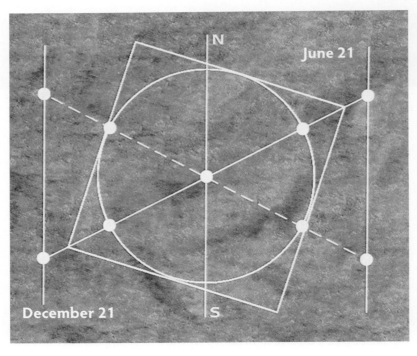

Figure 121

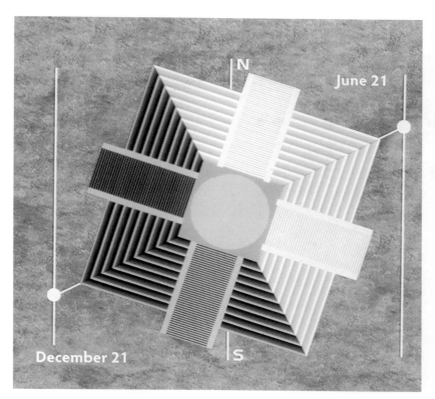

Figure 122

Figure 123

Figure 124

The entire thing is an ingenious demonstration of the highest astronomy and architecture in the sign of the gods. The message is crystal clear: the god Kukulkan descended from heaven. He stayed with the people for some time, taught them, and disappeared again to his starry home to return again at some point.

The Kukulkan pyramid of Chichén Itzá demonstrates how astronomers, mathematicians, architects, and priests entrusted their traditions to stone. It also proves that the entire theoretical knowledge, paired with the technical know-how, was present from the very beginning. There are no evolutionary trial runs of the pyramid, no permanent modifications and improvements. Even before the construction, the astronomical calculation had to be just as correct as the angle of inclination of the pyramid and the height of the nine platforms. A perfect stroke of genius created in the past for doubting people of the future.

The latest excavations demonstrate something amazing: The Kukulkan pyramid stands on a still more massive platform (figures 125 to 127). The entire structure, the giant foundation, must have already been there before the pyramid with the Kukulkan spectacle was built.

Figure 125

Figure 126

The fact that the Maya expected their gods to return is not only evident in the pyramid of Kukulkan in Chichén Itzá but also in Chilam-Balam book of Tizimin: "They arose from the streets with the stars behind them. . . . They spoke the magical language of the stars in the sky. . . . Yes, their sign is our certainty that they came from heaven . . . and when they descend from heaven again, they will rearrange what they once created."[25]

Figure 127

Figure 128

Nonstop Curiosities

On the Pacific coast of Guatemala, not far from Santa Lucia Cotzumalguapa, the clearing work done in 1860 brought some magnificent Mayan steles to light (today, they are known as the Bilbao monuments.) The native population did not think much of it because farmers repeatedly would encounter carved stones. News of the discovery reached the Austrian Dr. Habel, who explored the region in 1862, and had drawings made of the steles. He later showed them in Berlin to the director of the Ethnological Museum of Berlin at the time, Dr. Adolf Bastian (1826–1905). He was enthusiastic, and wanted to install the steles in his museum, and he traveled to Santa Lucia Cotzumalguapa in 1876. There, he bought the steles from the owner of the *finca* (farm) and contractually secured the rights to any future discoveries. But the trip from Guatemala to Berlin was arduous.

In the jungle terrain of Santa Lucia Cotzumalguapa there were neither flatbed wagons nor paved roads. A hastily summoned engineer suggested cutting the steles in half lengthwise and hollowing out the back sides. And so it happened. The behemoths were loaded on oxcarts and transported up to 80 kilometers (50 mi.) to the San José harbor. When loading them on the ship there was another hitch: One stele broke loose from its ropes and sank to the bottom of the harbor—where it lies to this day.

The remaining eight steles were erected in Berlin and can still be admired at the entrance to the local ethnological museum. One stele obviously shows an offering scene with a priest, who is holding a ripped-out heart to the heavens. In the next image, a priest stretches something upward that looks like a face mask. Above him a godly being, surrounded by flames, descends toward the earth (figure 128, page 144, and figures 129 to 131). The next image shows a figure engulfed in flames from the head downward. In front of its chest dangles a fire disc, and there, where the feet should be, rudiments of wings are recognizable.

Experts see these representations as an "ode to the sun god." This is more than lame. I ask you to compare figures 80 to 83 (pages 84–87) with figures 128 to 131. In both cases the winged figures plunge down toward the earth head and hands first. Figures 80 to 83 are from Tulum, a place on the Caribbean coast. There, the descending figures are called bee gods, and this, even though the shod feet of the figures rest on proper platforms. And the fiery flames? I am reminded of the Indian Maruts: "Come here, Marut, from the heavens, from the air. . . . Your brightly flashing men in the terrible missiles."

Figure 129

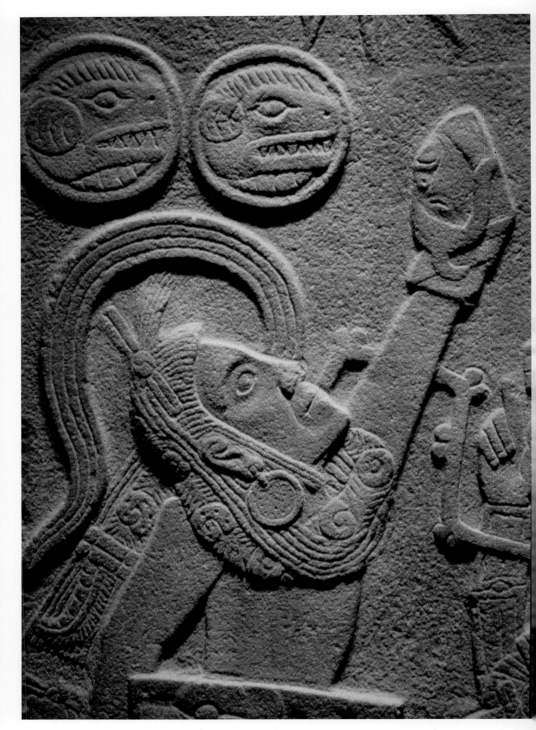

Figure 130

Figure 131

It is time to rethink some things. Because of so-called professional literature and our goal-oriented education we are blind in one eye. We accept what is offered in clever books and on the Internet, and we do not notice how we repress understanding. With that I am not stating that my approach is the only correct one. But the interpretation up until now is not exactly the final word.

Figure 132

Figure 133

    I saw a similar case of misunderstood technology in the statues of Tula, a place 70 kilometers (44 mi.) northwest of Mexico City. The figures—also known as Atlanteans, whatever that means— stand atop a pyramid-shaped platform (figures 132 and 133). They carry boxes on their chests, and even the harnesses over their shoulders are recognizable (figure 134). With two fingers, they clasp objects that look like drills and taper downward (figure 135). Half of a spoked wheel is also recognizable on their shoes (figure 136).

Figure 134

Figure 135

The experts' interpretation is completely different. The boxes on their chests are "butterfly symbols," the things in their hands are "a bundle of arrows" or "spinning devices," and the wheels on their shoes are supposedly "flowers." Then the covered ears could be—who knew it?—original headphones with a short antenna. Finally, the headdress in the eyes of the experts is a "box-shaped hat." Some of the Tula statues are even furnished on the backside with engravings. There stands an Indian adorned with a feathered helmet with a hose through the nose (figure 137) and a figure in squatting position. From head to back, a hose runs into a tank (figure 138). One can compare this with the stele of El Baúl in figure 26 (pages 26–27).

If the items of evidence are not an individual case, if they are seemingly waving from everywhere, if we are speaking about the mythology of "descended gods" and "teachers," if Teotihuacán turned out to be the model of the solar system and the Kukulkan pyramid of Chichén Itzá shows a light-and-shadow game year after year, as if this god descends the stairs, shouldn't the experts start pricking up their ears?

Which experts? The specialists on Maya archaeology? The few that have something to say can be counted on one hand. They travel without exception on their old tracks; new rails are frowned upon. And the diligent students cannot affect the switch position in any way, because they are only let in if they ride in the old train. Therefore, new thinking must come from the outside, even if it takes a generation to get attention. After all, the Maya experts do concede the existence of a prodigious astronomy in their studies—only the gods could never be visitors from other stars. One must understand all of this psychologically, it is said with emphatic nodding. And—curiously enough—the currently prevailing "politically correct" line of thought makes the professional immune to any type of contrarian thinking. If one would see the gods as actual extraterrestrials this would denigrate the achievement of the Indians: the pride of the Maya would be violated. This is obviously joined by the blessed doctrine of evolution.

Figure 136

Figure 137

Figure 138

People do not trouble themselves to understand another way of looking at things. Evolution, yes—but it does not explain everything. The statements by the experts ignore the fact that the temples and pyramids were built by people. And the remarkable pieces of art and mathematics were created by people. The initial impulse, however, came from outside. That is now verifiable, and the Maya say that themselves. The achievement of the people will not be devalued. The Berlin Symphony is not decreased when it plays *Rhapsody in Blue,* just because the composer George Gershwin was an American.

Figure 139

The Maya were addicted to astronomy. Their buildings and their religion, their entire spiritual thinking including their astronomically aligned pyramids, prove it. There are, at 1,500 meters (4,921 ft.) high, ruins at Xochicalco in the foothills of the Ajusco volcano in Mexico. For the temple up there, the Maya leveled off a mountaintop. The origin of Xochicalco is obscure, and up to now, only the half of all buildings have been unearthed. In the center is the stepped pyramid La Malinche and a so-called palace. Here, too, everything served astronomy. Two of the pyramids lie across from each other like mirror images (figures 139 to 140). The sun rises at the equinoxes exactly over the centers of the buildings.

Figure 140

Figure 141

Figure 142

La Malinche stands on a nearly square surface (18.6 × 21 m.; 61 × 68.9 ft.) and is aligned north-south. The outer wall carries magnificent reliefs of eight feathered snakes that wind themselves around the building as if they are trying to lift up the platform. On the other side of the world, in China, monsters were shown as flying dragons (figures 141, pages 160–61, and 142). The reliefs were cut with unidentified hard chisels directly in the andesite slabs and seamlessly joined together. Originally the pyramid must have glowed magnificently to the heavens, because paint residues are still stuck between the joints.

Ten meters (33 ft.) under the ground there is a room scraped out of the rock that people called an observatory, accessible through a side entry. From the ceiling of the room is a 9-meter (29.5 ft.) long shaft to the surface (figures 143 and 144). It is made so ingeniously that year after year, on June 21 at noon, a unique scenario replays itself.

At noon a small procession of Indians with lighted candles enters the room. They carry with them amulets and a small vessel of water, which is placed directly under the light shaft. Outside, the sun climbs higher, and exactly at 12:30 it stands in the center of the opening. Tentative at first, the beam of light glides along the walls as if searching; then the band of light broadens until it fills the shaft and illuminates the chamber underneath. Now the light engulfs the amulets and water tank on the ground, permeating them and causing them to reflect. Like luminous laser fingers they flash around and slowly pass over the people with their candles in their hands. This fascinating spectacle lasts approximately twenty minutes. The Indians, saying prayers, look to the shaft opening over them. As soon as the sun moves on it would become dark in the underworld if it were not for the flickering light of the small candles. The Indians take their amulets and water vessel that—according to their beliefs—are now animated with divine power, and walk silently outside. But then there is laughing, music, dancing, and expressions of gratitude for the divine power.

Figure 143

Figure 144

This occurs every year on June 21, even to this day. This sun cult reminds me of the Stone Age installation at Newgrange, 10,000 kilometers (6,214 mi.) away from Mexico in Ireland. Also occurring every year, and for a good 5,000 years now, is a similar spectacle, not on June 21, but on December 21. During the sunrise the blazing sun passes through a deliberately placed rectangular opening. The sunlight shines down a 24-meter (79 ft.) passageway and, like a laser beam, strikes a stone with various scraped out bowls. The rest is a magical symphony. The rays of light flicker in different directions, at all times directed precisely at cultic signs, but also above through a dead-straight and artfully made stone shaft. As in Xochicalco, Mexico.

Who actually devised this eccentric sunlight game? And it is not only in Mexico and Ireland. There are similar examples around the world. Who calculated the degree slope for the shafts for June 21 in Mexico and December 21 in Ireland? Were divine figures revered in the chambers? Did the astronomers construct their square shafts as a reference to the spectral colors of the rainbow? Were materials in the room treated so that they could only be seen in polarized light? Or was there some kind of luminescence down there that escaped the excavators?

I ask these (dumb) questions for a good reason, because objects of this type were reported three hundred years ago by the Spanish chronicler Francisco Antonio de Fuentes (and handed down by John Lloyd Stephens). This is in regard to the city of Patina Mit, the central city of the Cakchiquel Indians:

West of the city is a hill that towers above it, and on the hill a small, round building approximately 1.8 meters (5.9 ft.) tall. In the middle of this building is a pedestal made of a shimmering substance that looks like glass, but the true properties of this material are not known. Judges sit around this building and administer their judgments, which are immediately enforced. Before any enforcement was carried out, however, it was necessary that the judgment be verified through the oracle. For this purpose, three judges would leave their seats and betake themselves to a notch in the valley. There was the invocation site with a black, see-through stone, on whose surface the deity appeared and confirmed the verdict. If no apparition showed up on the black stone, the condemned person was immediately released. The same stone was consulted about decisions regarding war and peace. Later, Bishop Francisco Marroquin heard about this stone and ordered it smashed to pieces. The largest piece served as the altar plate of the church of Tecpan in Guatemala.[1]

Curious story. Had the Indians once seen the gods in something like a monitor and not understood anything? Over 175 years ago, both Mayan researchers Stephens and Catherwood sought the strange altar stone in the church of Tecpan, Guatemala—but the slab no longer existed. Someone had destroyed it.

Central America is a gold mine for fantasists, dreamers, and alternative thinkers—but between the fantasy and erstwhile reality is a narrow seam. Opinion can fluctuate on both sides. Presently, at the entrance to the Museo Popol Vuh in Guatemala City stand three massive skulls that cannot be attributed to anyone (figures 145 to 147). The eyes are oversized and the "eyeballs" are anything but eyeballs. In front of the nose a rectangular object is stuck—a massive filter? Ludicrous? As a globetrotter and expert on traditions I am put in mind of the Abraham Apocrypha, about whose existence Maya specialists don't need to know.

In that account, the boy Abraham experienced an extraterrestrial encounter. It is evening and Abraham is working in a field when two "heavenly beings" descend. Abraham specifies that they were "not people." If they were not human beings—then what? They both breathed, but not in the way humans breathe. Abraham is driven over the earth in a chariot of fire. He sees large figures whose words he did not understand, and heads toward a powerful light in the heavens, which he cannot describe. In the next sentence it is clear where Abraham was: "I wanted to fall down on the ground. The high place on which we were stood upright early on, but it soon turned downward."[2]

Figure 145

Figure 146

Figure 147

Figure 148

When a person wants "to fall down on the ground," he is hardly on the ground. In addition, the "high place" on which Abraham stands constantly rotates around its own axis. This is exactly what happens in a spaceship in orbit. Through self-rotation an inner artificial gravity is obtained. The centrifugal forces work similarly to a spin drier. But no one could have known this thousands of years ago. Therefore, my cross-connecting of the stone heads in the Museo Popol Vuh having square objects in front of their noses with Abraham's beings, who "did not breathe like humans." Still laughable? (And concerning this cross-connection, God knows it is not the only one.)

Figure 149

In the Museo Popol Vuh in Guatemala City are helmeted figures to marvel at, that one—coming from the perspective of cargo cults—could describe as "astronaut gods" (figure 148, pages 170–71, and figures 149 to 152). The connection to breathing "not in the way humans breathe" (Abraham) is obvious. And on the stele in figure 153, a god greets a priest. In the sky above is a carved figure that simultaneously sits and floats; in the upper right are the thighs with bent knees and legs pointed upward, and on the left the same figure with the shared upper body, this time seated. This matches the Indian prince in an old Mexican manuscript who flies together with his temple into the clouds (figure 154).

Figure 150

Figure 151

Figure 152

Figure 153

Figure 154

The painter Diego Rivera (1886–1957) created wide-ranging colorful frescoes in the government building of Mexico City that portrayed the lives of Indians before the arrival of the Spaniards. And here, the flying snake—the god Quetzalcoatl—with his pilot is not absent (figure 155). Traditions in word and image are the blurry memories of the people.

Figure 155

Anecdotal flying Indians supposedly still existed at the time of the Spanish conquerors. On March 3, 1524, Pedro de Alvarado battled in the highlands of Guatemala against a group of Quiché-Maya Indians. Something bewildering happened there: "The commander Tecum rose into the air and came flying, transformed into an eagle, covered in feathers, that grew on their own and were not applied artificially. He had wings that grew out of his body."[3]

Hocus-pocus? Apparently Captain Alvarado did not fall for any illusion, because the flying Indian pierced the body of Alvarado's horse with an obsidian spear. The Indian thought that the horse and man had grown together as one and that his lance would also kill the rider. This bafflement of the Indians was exploited by the Spaniards, and they stabbed the puzzled flyers.

True or legend? In any case, this place became the location of the encounter of Captain Alvarado and the flying Indian named Quetzaltenango. That is still the name of the Guatemalan city. And Guatemala City erected a monument to the flying Indian commander Tecum (figure 156). The figure wears a long, heavy feather coat.

Figure 156

Flying gods, fiery figures that plunge down from heaven, feathered snakes in the skies—although every Indian knew that snakes never fly—monstrous figures enveloped in rays, helmeted figures with "respirators," wings everywhere the eye can see, and a mythology full of celestial masters. And how do we smart-alecks get to be "creation's crowning glory," "the pinnacle of evolution," out of that? Nature religions. More thinking is not permitted.

I have the audacity to interpret expressions such as "thunder," "lightning," "heaven," "fire snakes," and so on, differently from what is allowed by the sacrosanct opinion from the lectern. There it is taught that primitive people did not understand natural forces and therefore deified what they did not understand. Obviously, there were nature religions, which do not need to be explained. But—cross my heart—do these natural forces talk, as they clearly do in the lore? Did they establish laws, show themselves to be teachers, explain the calendar to dumb people—with 365 days and to eight decimal places (counting the hours making the leap day)?

Did a natural phenomenon hand over the Ten Commandments to Moses, and did the lightning teach Enoch writing (before the Flood)? Were the early Maya referring to natural phenomena when they called teachers "great masters of the sciences"? Did thunder create people "according to its own image," and did the Maya align their temples astronomically only because lightning sometimes flashed from the skies in the north?

That the researchers and fluent translators of two generations ago did not come up with any other sensible interpretations is perhaps understandable. After all, none of our esteemed grandfathers knew anything about notions such as space travel and an inhabited universe. The old ideas made it into textbooks—where else?—clouding every modern finding since then. Yesterday's interpretations were once reasonable—today they are unreasonable. There are now far more realistic arguments for the meaning of creation myths, such as the approach of nature religions. I understand the persistence in academics of a certain fear that the acceptance of extraterrestrials could bring about the collapse of a familiar way of looking. The collapse of a mindset is not the purpose for this book. The legitimation for a change in thinking comes from the new way of looking at things. Science is a living edifice and not a religion that one has to believe. "To realize that one made a mistake is only the admission that one is smarter today than yesterday," stated Jonathan Caspar Lavater (1741–1801). No one should feel embarrassed about taking leave of an outdated view. Among such is included the undying opinion that the Maya did not know what a wheel was. Why, then, did they build paved roads?

Thanks to countless satellite images, it is long known that Maya cities were connected to each other through an extensive network of roads. Sixteen of these roads began (or ended) in Cobá in the north of the current state of Quintana Roo. A long loop is formed by a road from Cobá to Yaxuaán, a small place not far from the ruins of Chichén Itzá. Aerial images show light bands in the dark green vegetation of the jungle. That is the road from Cobá, which runs by way of Yaxuná, Chichén Itzá, and Mayapán to Uxmal. That equals a highway of 300 kilometers (186 mi.). Another road connects Dzibilchaltún (before Mérida) with the eastern coast of the Caribbean. All roads were paved with small stones and coated with a light surface. The stretch from Cobá to Yazuná is 10 meters (33 ft.) wide—relatively grandiose for a processional route; fifteen people could have sung side by side.

The roads are often divided into ruler-straight sections, the longest of which measures 36 kilometers (22 mi.), and long-drawn stretches with numerous direction changes, which is no different from our highways. And the Maya were not familiar with the wheel?!

Then why does the Museum of Xalapa have a Mayan children's toy with wheels (figure 157)? Why can one find in the National Museum of Anthropology in Mexico City figures that operate a wheel with their legs (figure 158)? The other wheels have hubs (figures 159 and 160). And obviously the world-renowned calendar of the Aztecs is round (figure 161). At some point, stonemasons noticed that round blocks could roll. In addition, the curve or circle was already known to the Maya. Figures 162 and 163 from the garden of the museum at Xalapa could serve as examples.

Figure 157

Figure 158

Figure 159

Figure 160

Figure 161

Today's roads are planned to the foot. How did the Maya solve this problem? They supposedly did not have compasses. What surveying tools were used? Was the planning worked out with the help of beacons? The area is as flat as a frying pan and overgrown with dense forest. There are no small hills from which signs could be given. A fire in a green thicket is only visible for a few kilometers. Were people sent ahead to draw tight, straight lines and then mark the segment with stakes? Possibly. But this solution assumes that lanes were previously beaten through the jungle. At some point somebody must have decided how many miles of the way should run straight and when an elongated curve should be followed. This is not very easy in a forested area with a visibility of at best only two kilometers. Furthermore, in the flat terrain of the Maya there were small hollows, watercourses, depressions, and indeed swamps. The Maya leveled them, built, where needed, arched overpasses and raised sections of road up to five meters (16 ft.) high. Everything to excess on the procession routes. The

Figure 162

Figure 163

pilgrims would have traveled over the hollows without complaint. Today, we use steamrollers to press the roads flat. And the Maya? A five-ton roller broken into two parts was located in Ekal on the Cobá-Yaxuná route. These 4-meter (13 ft.) long rollers had a hub in the middle through which an axle once passed. But they did not know about the wheel.

Why else would the Maya level their roads if not for the wheel? Why did they build roads over marshy terrain with such solid foundations that they still have not sunk, even today? What would have traveled over these masterfully planned roads? Sleds with wooden runners? They would have left tracks in the surface. Did the Maya drive pack and draft animals on the roads with them? The consensus is that the Maya knew of neither. Did fast couriers with roller skates make their way on the roads? It is not impossible, because carved on the so-called Palacio in the Mayan city of Palenque is a roller skater (figures 164 and 165). "That's not true!" exclaim the experts. Said "rollers" mean nothing more than the number two. And that, even though little wheels are clearly seen under the front toe and under the sole of the foot, as

Figure 164

the pictures show! In addition, the buckles firmly fastened to the ankles are also recognizable. So these are nothing but sandals with the number two under them? And if the Maya really moved off the ground, then they would have no need for any roads. Something has escaped our cleverly deductive archaeologists.

These Maya and their predecessors must have been more construction mad than the ancient Egyptians. Always in honor of their flying god Quetzalcoatl emerged pyramids more extensive than the Great Pyramids of Giza. One hundred years ago, on top of a grassy hill in Cholula stood the church of Nuestra Señora de los Remedios (Our Lady of Remedies). The Spaniards did not build the church because of its beautiful view of the majestic Mount Popocatépetl, but because they wanted to hide a pagan Maya pyramid. Actually, the pyramid of Cholula, with its base length of 450 × 450 meters (1,476 × 1,476 ft.) and a height of 66 meters (216.5 ft.), has a larger volume than the Pyramid of Cheops. It's estimated that 4.5 million cubic meters of construction materials are contained in it (figure 166). Terraces of a step pyramid came to the fore, thirty-six stairways going in different directions and—

Figure 165

Figure 166

gasp!—to date a tunnel 5.5 kilometers (3.4 mi.) long (figures 167 to 172). Official doctrine says that the construction began in the second century CE and that it was raised in multiple stages. The layout—and its age—was compared to the enormous complex of Teotihuacán on the edge of Mexico City. I believe the origins of Teotihuacán lie much further in the past, and are equal to that of Cholula. Already the piles of rubble that have grown over it testify to this (compare the debris in figure 167).

The same goes for the phenomenal installation of Monte Albán, located 550 kilometers (341.8 mi.) southeast of Mexico City at a height of 1,950 meters (1.2 mi.). These ruins are today considered a World Heritage Site by UNESCO. As elsewhere, the builders first leveled a mountain, all of this prior to 3,000 years ago, because the origin of Monte Albán dates back at least to 1000 BCE. The founders of this holy site were supposedly Olmecs, the bearers of that puzzling culture that created the massive, helmeted skulls found in Olmec Park in Villahermosa (figure 88, page 92).

Figure 167

Figure 168

Figure 169

Figure 170

Figure 171

Figure 172

And, in the same park, the figure descending to the people as well as the dark-skinned one who stares toward the heavens in amazement are also Olmec (figures 90 to 92 on pages 94–97). These Olmecs founded Monte Albán. In their ranks, there must have been geniuses of planning. Who else had the idea 3,000 years ago to level a mountain, and this on a giant surface area (figures 173 to 177)? Apparently, the planners reckoned that later generations would fortify their work and would keep to the established astronomical

Figure 173

Figure 174

orientation—which is what happened. But the geographical point of Monte Albán was not randomly chosen. The relevant legend tells about a mysterious creator being named Coqui Xee, who slept in a hole in the grotto of "endless time."[4] Coqui Xee stood outside of the world because thoughts could not affect him. But on the inside he carried the wish to experience our world. And so Coqui Xee (who could not be affected by thoughts) gave birth to himself as light and began his long journey as light in the sky. He created people and Xonaxi, who transformed himself into a parrot in order to wander the sky. In order not to get lost, Xonaxi painted his path with light. This light trail was named the Milky Way by the Indians. And because Xonaxi descended on Monte Albán, it became the point of sacred ground. Therefore the founding of Monte Albán. The name Monte Albán goes back to the Zapotec word *danibaan* and means "sacred mountain."

Two thousand years ago, Monte Albán was already one of the largest cities of Mesoamerica with a population of 20,000.[5] As discoveries confirm, there were high-ranking contacts between Monte Albán and the pyramid city of Teotihuacán. People exchanged ideas and goods—in the end, Teotihuacán was similarly a place of the gods like Monte Albán. The buildings on the sacred mountain were enveloped in bright colors. At first, the buildings were covered with a white stucco layer and then painted, and the stairways were covered with a layer of red mortar. On forty large relief panels excavators found strange figures engraved in stone. One can recognize naked men and beasts in partly twisted poses with crossed and open legs; then again with mutilated genitalia or spread thighs (figures 178 to 183). Previously, the representations were called dancers, but today it is difficult to find a designation for them. And in the midst of them the image of an elephant, but that wouldn't make sense (figures 184 and 185). There were no elephants in America, so no one would have recognized the elephant in the relief of the devil—even if it is one. Out of the trunk, birds with overhanging lips and peculiar parrots are conjured. Elephants in America—impossible?

Figure 175

Figure 176

Figure 177

Figure 178

And what if one of the "gods" took one of his students to Asia and brought him back? Laughable? At the very least, Indian legends give an account of this. And in India the elephant god Ganesh is honored. In most Indian temples one can find a stone carved with Ganesh. They do not look very different from the pachyderm on Monte Albán.

Every day, the Voladores, the four mast-flying Indians, demonstrate their flight art on Monte Albán. Still today the godly game is regularly played on the ball field of Monte Albán, where the players no longer have to use a heavy five-pound hard rubber ball as before.

But I can't stop thinking of that odd mythological being named Coqui Xee, who supposedly slept in the hole of the grotto of "endless time." Coqui Xee was finally the reason for the sanctuary on Monte Albán. This Coqui Xee should have stood outside the world, because thoughts could not touch him. He himself traveled through the heavens. Hearing such legends, several cross-connections flash in my mind, though from completely different cultures. Exactly this makes the tradition exciting. Why do people separated from one another know synonymous stories? Would you care for examples?

Figure 179

Figure 180

Figure 181

On the island of Raivavae in French Polynesia, the old temple Te Mahara still stands as the point on which the god Maui landed after his flight in outer space.[6] The same applies to the ancient inhabitants of Atu Ona, a small island in the Marquesas. There the mountain Kei An is considered a temple, although no building stands on the spot. The ancient Polynesians named it Mount Tautini-Etua, which literally translated means "mountain on which the gods landed."[7]

Regarding the creator god Ta'aroa from the Society Islands of the Pacific: "Ta'arora sat in his shell in darkness since eternity. The shell was like an egg that floats in endless space. There was no sky, no ocean, no moon, no sun, no stars. Everything was dark."[8]

And in Samoa, it was reported about the original god Tagaloa: "God Tagaloa swam in the void, he created everything. Before him, there was no sky, no land, and he was all alone and slept in the expanse of space. His name was Tagaloafa'atutupunu'u, which means 'origin of growth.'"[9]

The creation myth of Kiribati (Micronesia, Pacific) begins with the establishment long, long ago given by the god Nareau.[10] No one knew where he came from, because Nareau flew alone and slept in space. In sleep, he heard his name be called three times, although the one who called his name was a "nobody." Nareau awoke and looked around. There was nothing but emptiness, but a large object was under him. It was Te-Bomatemaki—which means "earth and heaven together."

In the east Colombian highlands the Cordillera lived as a tribe of Chibcha. The Spanish historian Pedro Simon chronicled their creation legend: "It was night. But there were other things in the world. The light was locked in a large 'something house' and came out of it. This 'something house' is *chiminigagua* and it contained the light in itself, that it might come out. In the light of the light, things began to be."[11]

And the creation account in presumably the oldest book of humanity, the Indian Rig Veda, puts us doubters again in the state of weightlessness and silence:

> There was neither non-being nor being then. There was neither the realm of space nor the sky beyond. What stirred back and forth? What was the unfathomable? . . . There was neither death nor immortality then. There was no sign of day or night. The One breathed according to its own law, without wind. Other than that was nothing there. . . . Was there a below? Was there an above? . . . Who knows for sure, who can proclaim it, whence they came, whence the creation?[12]

Figure 182

Figure 183

Figure 184

I could draw out this play of comparisons much longer—and time and again familiar elements would appear. Coqui Xee, the real founder of the sanctuary on Monte Albán, slept "in a hole in the grotto of endless time." He came from "outside of the world," slept somewhere endlessly long, and "thoughts could not affect him." The synonymity with other myths is obvious.

Figure 185

In Costa Rica there is actually a puzzle that connects the inhabitants with the "balls in the sky." In that Central American country there are around three hundred stone spheres made from gabbro, a granitelike plutonic rock. Only isolated spheres of shale or sandstone are extant. Most of the stone balls are symmetrically circular, with diameters ranging from 10 centimeters (3.9 in.) to 2.48 meters (8.1 ft.). People found and still find them

Figure 186

in the Diquis Delta on the Pacific side of Guatemala, but also in Rio Esquina National Park, on the mountaintops, and today even in open places of Guatemala City (figures 186 to 188). In Golfo Dulce fifteen of the giant balls lie in a perfectly straight line; north of the Sierra Brunquera, near the village of Uvita, twelve balls; in the muddy bed of the Esquina River appeared four balls—no one knows how many have been washed away over the

Figure 187

millennia. On Camaronal Island, people discovered two of these balls, and more "sky balls"—as they were called—lie on the peaks of Cordillera Brunquera. How in the world did they get all the way up there? Guatemala was primeval forest. The balls could not easily roll around. For rolling routes, people would have had to cut through the jungle. The same is true for the forested mountain slopes, where even the strongest of arms would not be enough to roll up the tons-heavy balls. Cables would have been essential.

As the United Fruit Company began to clear the virgin forest to create banana plantations in the 1930s, the engineers repeatedly met with unnatural resistance in the ground. The old steam

Figure 188

Figure 189

bulldozers of the time uncovered the stone spheres, and the workers pushed the unwanted things aside while shaking their heads. Then the aptly named Doris Stone, the daughter of an engineer, rode for weeks from one find to the next and wrote the first report about the incomprehensible spheres of Costa Rica. The first black-and-white photos are from her (figure 189).[13] Stone closed her work with the resigned observation: "The balls of Costa Rica must be considered as one of the unsolved megalithic mysteries of the world."

Today, we are no further along. We do not know who created the stone balls, we do not know with which tools and geometric aids they worked, we do not know for what purpose the balls were created, nor when it happened. Everything that has been suggested is completely speculative. A local legend suggests that the balls represent the sun. But the sun was represented by the Indians as a golden disk, a rayed wheel, or even as a discus—not as a sphere. If it were so, the Indians would have had their "sun balls" painted a golden color. There are no paint residues. In contrast to the smaller ones, all the large balls are literally spherical with smoothly polished surfaces. How did Stone Age people do that?

Did the stonemasons first of all have the raw material—a stone block—that was buried in the ground and then commence shaving it all around, which would inevitably create inaccuracy, since the distances to the parts of the stone stuck in the ground could no longer be controlled. But the raw materials must have come from somewhere. There are no quarries in the places they were found. And why would the finished balls be transported to any old location, and sometimes to the height of a mountain? One theory holds that the balls were simply rolled through the riverbeds. The riverbeds are muddy and pebbly. The heavy stone balls sank. But the "riverbed theory" cannot explain balls on the mountains.

Experts believe that to produce a stone ball that weighs fifteen tons, the raw materials must have weighed at least twenty-four tons. In the face of three hundred balls, one can imagine the amount of raw material that must have been moved. In addition, there are multiple heavier balls on opposite sides of some rivers (figure 190). This means that there were considerable barriers to material transport. Without flatbeds, without roads, without cranes, without cargo ships—and all in the jungle. In the Museo Popol Vuh in Guatemala City, I asked an archaeologist about the significance of the balls. "Perhaps religious or ritual background," he said shrugging. "Possibly also some sky cult."

Cults, as far as the eye can see: on statues, temples, pyramids. Most of them honor gods. Which gods?

Figure 190

Figure 191

Figure 192

King Pakal's Ascension

Located in the southern Mexican state of Chiapas, Palenque has a unique role for any observers wearing cargo-cult specs. For the (by now) world-famous tombstone is in Palenque: a 3.8-meter (12.5 ft.) long and 2.2-meter (7.2 ft.) wide monolith with various representations and Mayan characters. For experts, there are no open questions about the representations on the slab. Everything follows a compulsory logic within Maya research. Lay people, however, recognize in the reliefs something extraterrestrial: misunderstood technologies.

I wrote about the history of Palenque twenty-five years ago[1] and must do it once more (again: willingly or reluctantly). Without some repetition I would leave new readers out in the cold.

It was in 1773 in the town of Tumbala. A Spanish expeditionary force reported to the curator of the district, Mr. Antonio de Solis, that some *casas de piedras* (stone houses) were located in the nearby jungle. Antonio de Solis, a priest, did not take the report as very important. Primitive Indian buildings were everywhere. The news about the *casas de piedras* also reached the priest Ramon Ordoñez, who still hoped, maybe somewhere, to dig up a treasure. Ordoñez put together a small group that found the stone houses close to the village of Santo Domingo de Palenque and reported about pyramids, halls, and towers.

This report reached the royal commission "Audiencia" in Guatemala, which in turn posted Colonel Antonio del Rio there to watch more closely the *casas de piedras*. With him went a draftsman who could record what lay in the jungle. From Santo Domingo de Palenque to the ruins were a laughable 6 kilometers (3.7 mi.). But the thickness of the jungle and the rainy season made the path through the green hell an adventure. On May 3, 1787, Colonel Antonio del Rio reached the *casas de piedras* with his squad. And with that began the discovery of Palenque.

Colonel del Rio needed two weeks to thin out the brush around the buildings and cut through the foliage. Then he "stood in the middle of a clearing and stared spellbound at the ruins of a palace, a true maze of rooms and courtyards, high on a giant platform made of earth and rubble"[2] (figures 191 and 192, page 216). The walls were covered with unintelligible signs and mysterious figures, and rainwater dripped from countless gutters. Swarms of bloodthirsty mosquitos bit the men through their shirts. Colonel del Rio wanted to get his sweat-soaked assignment behind him as quickly as possible and had the floors ripped up and walls torn down. His actions still astound archaeologists to this day.

Nonetheless, del Rio brought thirty-two objects and twenty-five drawings to Santo Domingo de Palenque, which were passed on to the Audiencia. The dossier traveled at some point to Madrid, and there all crates with their drawings disappeared into an insatiable archive. The heap of rubble in New Spain, as the conquered regions were known back home, did not interest anyone in the royal court.

But sometimes chance rules. Forty-five years later, del Rio's report inexplicably landed in the hands of London bookseller Henry Berthoud. He liked what he saw and in 1822 published a small booklet with some drawings from del Rio's report. This booklet in turn fascinated an amiable and colorful character: the Count Johann Friedrich von Waldeck. It is not documented where this Count Waldeck came from. He himself offered various curricula vitae to the world. He sometimes gave his birthplace as Paris, once as Prague, once as Vienna. Whoever he was, Waldeck was an outstanding draftsman. And he made up his mind to travel to Palenque.

In March of 1822 Waldeck set off from London. He left his family behind. Before leaving he had a fund-raising campaign for his expedition to Palenque that barely brought in anything. The word *Palenque* meant nothing to anyone. In Mexico Waldeck actually managed to receive official approval to carry out research in Palenque. So he invited the Indians of Santo Domingo de Palenque to help him in the name of the Mexican government to excavate the ruins. But the Indians wanted to see money—they didn't care about any far-off government. Waldeck's entire belongings consisted of 3,000 Mexican dollars that melted away like butter in the blazing sun. Completely broke, he still continued on. Often left alone, tormented by the tropical environment, he made his way to the overgrown temples, sat day after day, drawing board on his knees, in the sultry heat and captured Palenque in more than 100 drawings. In order to escape the diluvian cloudbursts and the furiously biting insects, Count Waldeck set up a modest camp in a ruin that he separated from the outdoors with a curtain. Today, the building is affectionately and mockingly called the Temple of the Count.

Waldeck's enthusiasm never waned. In specific reliefs he thought he discovered elephant heads, and he believed that Palenque must have been reached by people from Africa or Asia. Today's experts see Waldeck's elephants as "masks of rain gods." Waldeck raged when locals dared to break the plaster panels from the walls in order to sell them. He jealously observed foreign visitors, because he hated when others sketched "his" building. Bitter and destitute, Waldeck traveled to Campeche in the spring of 1834. There he hoped to sell his drawings for a hefty price.

But in the meantime the government in Mexico City was replaced, and Waldeck did not trust the new rulers. So he had all his drawings copied in pencil. He trusted the originals to a British official who brought them to London. Suddenly, the Mexican newspapers accused Count Waldeck of living as a vandal in Palenque and secretly taking away treasures. None of this was true. A delegation of the mayor had Waldeck's baggage searched and confiscated his drawings. They were the copies.

Angry and disappointed, Waldeck left Mexico and moved with his family to their quarters in Paris. In 1838 he published the memories of his romantic archaeological journey in Yucatán with a selection of twenty-one drawings that were his favorites. And so began another round for Palenque.

In New York at that time lived the lawyer John Lloyd Stephens, who had a passion for traveling. The jurist had visited different countries in Europe, and also Turkey, Palestine, and Egypt. To his acquaintances back home, Stephens sent humorously perceptive and spicy letters—without knowing that one of his American friends would publish these letters. And so the lawyer Stephens, without his consent, became the travel writer Stephens. In London he visited the exhibition "Panorama Jerusalem" with a series of pictures by the well-known painter Frederick Catherwood. Stephens sought to make contact with Catherwood, whose work deeply touched him. They met in a London tearoom. Catherwood was also well-traveled and possessed entire maps full of interesting drawings with temple motifs from the Mediterranean. Their shared wanderlust and adventures in far continents made them friends. Where should they go?

Just at that time the booklet with Count Waldeck's drawings was circulating in London. Stephens and Catherwood at first doubted whether the forests of Mexico actually had such remarkable ruins. And if so, they could never come from the Indians or their ancestors. The new friends were determined to travel to Central America and get to the bottom of things. At first Stephens returned to New York and became active as a lawyer. He applied for the post of diplomatic representative of the United States at the head office of Latin American countries in Guatemala. Luckily, relationships and his degree of notoriety as travel writer worked in his favor. Stephens became the diplomat, and received his desired passport and a pile of letters of recommendation. With those it was possible for him to charge the state with part of his travel costs. He then met Frederick Catherwood in New York. Stephens gave him a contract as the expedition artist and secured continuous maintenance payments for the Catherwood family. On October 3, 1839, the friends set off. Destination: the controversial ruins of an unknown culture of Central America.

There were two long, adventurous journeys in which Stephens and Catherwood visited, described, and drew forty-four ruined cities. In 1841 and 1843, Stephens published his reports, which hit the wider scientific world like a bomb.[3]

The tourists that drive to the superbly restored ruins in an air-conditioned bus know nothing of the tribulations Stephens and Catherwood endured some 170 years before. The rainy season had just begun as the friends, accompanied by some inhabitants from the nearby village of Santo Domingo de Palenque, reached the ruins. The jungle dripped and steamed. The *casas de piedras* were twisted under the dense jungle and mosses, and so they did not find them at first. Just like Count Waldeck, they had no choice but to establish quarters in the first ruin they found. After the mosquitos turned their first night into hell under a ruined roof, all of their possessions got wet; in the humidity of the continuous rain their shoes, clothes, and the leather gear began to mildew, iron devices such as spades and blades began to rust. Always full of humor, Stephens noted: "We considered ourselves already securely booked for rheumatism."

Stephens paid his workers eighteen cents per day, but they were lazy, came too late, and left early: "Sometimes only two or three showed up, and the same Indian rarely came a second time, so that during our stay, all the Indians of a village rotated through us." The mosquitos, "those murderers of rest," joined along with poisonous snakes, ticks, and other parasites. The nights were dreadful. They could not light any candles, because the light would bring the pests by the thousands. Only the smoke of cigars kept the critters at a distance.

After they finally fought through the brush and lianas to a pyramid, they discovered broken stones or walls: the work of Colonel del Rio. Stephens discovered more locations where reliefs were obviously removed by profiteers to be sold. Then they stood overwhelmed in front of the walls from which grim faces peered. Proud sad-looking statues commanded respect: "We were fixed with wonder by their expressions of serene composure and their strong similarity to Egyptian statues." Despite the recollection of Egypt, Stephens was aware of the uniqueness of the culture of the people that had built Palenque: "What we saw was marvelous, puzzling, and very remarkable." He wrote that nothing "in world history books impressed him as much as this spectacular, large, and lovely city." Wrapped in humorous conversational style, Stephens delivered proof of his expertise and his brilliant powers of observation. Catherwood's illustrations completed the work with precise representations of the buildings and sculptures. Catherwood was "the first illustrator who accepted Mayan art in its own style."[4] Even today, Catherwood's images are irreplaceable because the level of detail worked out in his fine strokes cannot be achieved with photography. In addition, the images show things that disappeared long ago. Stephens and Catherwood deserve the credit for "having opened the era of scientific Maya research."[5]

In their time Stephens and Catherwood could only guess and speculate. The Mayan writing was not yet deciphered, and the Mayan calendar was not yet known. A Popul Vuh—the "bible" of the Quiché Maya—was not yet read by anyone, not to mention the Chilam Balam books or the old Mexican manuscripts. But at the time, it was clear to both researchers that it was a matter of religion and of gods—but the meanings of them, the resulting confusion, first began 120 years later.

The origin of Palenque is still not known today. The word *Palenque* comes from the Spaniards who used it to describe the wooden enclosures and the dwellings of the Indians. The history of the Maya, however, can be read in many temples, especially the Temple of the Inscriptions. According to that, on March 11, 431 CE, a thirty-four-year-old monarch named Bahlum Kuk ascended the throne. This was followed by a dynasty of ten generations, in which the boy Pakal occupied a critical role. This Pakal inherited the throne from his mother, and the accession was imposed upon him when he was barely twelve years old. He ruled sixty-eight years and was finally buried in the famous pyramid named the Temple of the Inscriptions. More on that later.

No building in Palenque is in its location by chance; everything has to do with astronomy and the cosmos. In addition to the "Palace," the group of "Temples of the Cross"—actually smaller pyramids—is predominant, where each temple stands for a heavenly ruler (figures 193 and 194). Since the German Maya researcher Heinrich Berlin did not understand the gods of these temples, he labeled them with numbers: God I, God II, and God III.[6] That is what they are still called today (figures 195 and 196). From the inscriptions on the Temple of the Cross, we know the birth date of God I: October 21, 2360 BCE.

Figure 193

Figure 194

Figure 195

Figure 196

Figure 197

Figure 198

As in Egypt and India, naturally God I was originally "descended from heaven."⁷ God II (with the name K'awii) shows up in the Temple of the Foliated Cross. He was the youngest of the three divinities. Yet his birthday is millennia in the past: born on November 8, 2360 BCE. God III is the sun god, and his temple is the sun temple. He was born—according to the inscriptions—on October 25, 2360, so in the same year as God I and God II. All three buildings of the Cross Temple Group represent in their arrangement the cosmology and royal power.

At present, the most prominent Mayan writing experts are father and son David and George Stuart (University of Texas, Austin). Both were critically involved in deciphering Mayan writing and are undisputed top experts of the field. They believe that the general theme of the Temple of Palenque is the rebirth of the gods in heaven. "We see that the three temples together symbolize the bases of the cosmos: the heaven, the water surface, and the underworld. It is no accident: the Temple of the Cross is the highest, the Temple of the Sun is the lowest, and the Temple of the Foliated Cross symbolizes the middle"[8] (figure 197, pages 226–27, and figures 198 and 199).

Figure 199

Did the three gods create the universe? Were they something like the Holy Trinity of the Christian religion (Father, Son, and Holy Spirit)? No, there were ancestors to these gods that, logically, must have been older than Gods I, II, and III. In the inaugural panel of the Temple of the Cross, a goddess appears from the year 3121 BCE, and in Temple XIX, we learn that God I assumed his royal office in 3309 BCE. King of what? Of Palenque? No. The inscription in Temple XIX clearly shows that it deals with a reign "in heaven." At some point, people must have argued about the notion of "heaven."

With the confusing data from the world of the Maya gods comes the question: Is all this real? Was this truly meant? Where do the exact dates of birth come from: Are they inventions or wishful thinking by the Maya priests? Were some type of beings actually born in heaven on those named dates? Or was there before Palenque, as some archaeologists are investigating, already another "Palenque," another much older city, and do the dates of birth refer to this unknown place? No archaeological evidence has been discovered that would justify there being a Palenque before Palenque. Or—asked speculatively—is the data concerning various gods providing true data that can be understood only in connection with space travel? (Meanwhile, it has long been proved that for astronauts in a very fast spaceship, time passes differently than for the inhabitants of the starting planet.)

As a vagabond between cultures it is my job to draw the attention of the experts on the Maya to the fact that preposterous dates are passed down in areas of the world completely different from Central America. From Babylonia comes a 20.5 centimeter (8 in.) high stone block, called WB 444 (located today in the British Museum), on which the reigning years of the oldest kings before the Flood were listed.

As the kingdom descended from heaven
Was the kingdom in Eridu.
In Eridu was Alulim king
He ruled 28,800 years . . .
Illta-sadum
Ruled 1,200 years
Mes-kiag-ga (ser)
Son of the sun god
1,324 years
He ruled
The divine Lugal-banda
1,200 years
He ruled . . .

And it continues, one and a half pages long. And exactly these "crazy" dates were given by the ancient historian Diodorus. He wrote: "At first, gods and heroes ruled Egypt for a little less than 18,000 years. And the last divine king was Horus, son of Isis. But the land was ruled by human kings from Moeris for no less than 5,000 years, to the 180th Olympiad, which is when I myself traveled to Egypt."[9]

Manetho, another historian who was active in Egypt centuries ago, claimed: "After the gods, the lineage of divine offspring ruled for 1,255 years. And in turn, other kings ruled for 1,817 years. Then came thirty kings, Memphites, ruling for 1,790 years . . . and then the kingdom of divine offspring for 5,813 years."[10]

And this goes on, whether in Egypt, Babylon, India, Tibet, or even in the Old Testament. Adam is supposed to have been 930 years old, Seth 912 years old, Methuselah 969 years old, and so on. I am not baffled by these dates of the Maya. As in the creation myths, there is a reality hidden behind the impossible

Figure 200

numbers. Our present problem is the specialization of certain disciplines. Maya scholars mostly do not know anything about the date of "WB 444" or those of Diodorus. We all live only one life and it is too short to be specialists in multiple fields.

The third table of the Temple of Inscriptions of Palenque even turns up a date that is connected with the "boy king Pakal," which is 1,247,654 years in the past. On top of that: The Mayan writing experts David and George Stuart draw attention to the fact that in Palenque, future dates were projected: "Pakal's evident 'timelessness' was highlighted on a table by his renewed resurrection (appearance) 4,000 years in the future."[11]

The dates are there, carved into stone. And while we have to put everything in order, we bundle our thoughts according to the logic of the zeitgeist. What else? Will future generations possibly laugh about our logic?

Deep in the ground under the pyramid that is called the Temple of Inscriptions lies the grave of the ruler K'inich Janaab Pakal. He was the greatest ruler of Palenque and his building is another story (figure 200). It lies in the southwest corner of the so-called Palace and sits atop a 16-meter (52.5 ft.) tall pyramid made of nine plinths piled on top of one another. In 1949 the Mexican archaeologist Dr. Alberto Ruz Lhuillier worked as the chief excavator in Palenque. He was most interested in the Temple of Inscriptions, because his predecessors barely dug there. One day he noticed a rectangle on the floor of the upper platform, where the inscriptions were stuck to the walls. By uncovering a panel, the edge of a stairway step became visible. Obviously, the stairway led into the inner pyramid, although it was stuffed with stones and mud. The work was torture. The deeper the diggers penetrated, the more compact the mud was and therefore the heavier the rocks. Stone after stone was hoisted up by the men, every bucket with mud was individually carried out. Twenty-three steps were finally freed. Alberto Ruz was convinced that the work would end in the coming year and the secrets of the pyramid would be revealed.

In the next excavating season, twenty-one additional steps were freed from the dreck. But who hid something there and intentionally filled it back in millennia ago (figure 201)? Finally,

Figure 201

Figure 202

Figure 203

at the forty-fifth step within the pyramid, the ground became flat and made a U-turn. But then the stairway continued in the eastern direction. A year later, the men burrowed deeper. Then a rectangular hole appeared in a wall, and the diggers could literally breathe. The opening turned out to be a ventilation shaft that ran through an 8-meter (26 ft.) thick wall on the western side of the pyramid.

In 1952 a new obstacle of stone and mortar prevented all progress. The sweat-dripping Sisyphean task in the damp, hot pyramid would not end. After some steps the diggers stood before a 4-meter (13 ft.) thick wall. There they found the bones of a sacrificed youth. On June 15, 1952, Dr. Ruz stood with his team before a triangular door (figures 202 and 203). With a chisel, it was nudged a handsbreadth to the side. Dr. Ruz held a flashlight through the opening and pressed his face to the moist slab. Breathless, he described to his team what he saw: "At first I noticed a large, empty room, a type of ice cave, whose walls and ceiling seemed to me to be perfect surfaces, like an abandoned chapel, from whose ceiling entire curtains of stalactites hung. As if they were thick, dripping candles."[12]

The walls, on which colorful reliefs with figures were stuck, glistened like snow crystals. The floor of the crypt was covered by a single almost 4-meter (13 ft.) long slab that was entirely covered with glyphs. As the triangular door was opened enough to let the men through, the stalactites (dripstones) were knocked from the ceiling out of impatience and curiosity in the excitement of the moment. What a shame! If only a single stalactite remained, just how old this subterranean room was could have been calculated. Dripstones get bigger year after year by some millimeters or centimeters, depending on whether the water is dripping through lime or granite layers. The crypt under the pyramid is 9 meters (29.5 ft.) long, 4 meters (13 ft.) wide, and 7 meters (23 ft.) tall. It would have rained over Palenque for centuries, millennia, and water penetrated through the masonry. As long as the temple city was active, the Maya maintained their sanctuaries, and cracks in the buildings were patched with mortar. In addition, the buildings glowed in bright colors. Just a little water trickled though the cracks into the subterranean room. Only when Palenque was uninhabited did fissures form in the pyramid's outer layer, and plant seeds could settle in these gaps and break the stones.

Figure 204

Figure 205

The discovered room lay 2 meters (6.6 ft.) under the base of the Temple of Inscriptions (= pyramid). The hieroglyphic plate on the floor proved to be a single monolith, 3.8 meters (12.5 ft.) long and 2.2 meters (7.2 ft.) wide, 25 centimeters (9.8 in.) thick and weighing around 8 tons (figure 204). Under the slab is a sarcophagus (figure 205). It was quickly clear that this "tombstone," as it is called today, could never have been transported through the narrow staircase to the inside of the pyramid. The room with the slab existed before the pyramid: first came the subterranean crypt and later the building above.

Since the discovery by Alberto Ruz Lhuillier, sixty years have passed, in which different meanings have been given to the remarkable relief on the slab (I first show the image in horizontal, figure 206, and later in vertical format, figure 209). The discoverer, Alberto Ruz, believed it was about

Figure 206

a young man, retreating behind a large mask of the earth monster. . . . Over his body stands a cross, identical with the famous cross of another temple in Palenque. Out of a double-headed snake spring small mythological shapes, on top a Quetzal bird with the mask of the rain god. We can accept that the scene represents fundamental concepts of the Mayan religion.[13]

The American Herbert Wilhelmy recognized in the central figure the corn god Yum Kox.[14] Pierre Ivanoff disagreed:

The symbolic meaning of this curious representation poses some puzzles. The god of death, with his connection to the underworld, is, according the beliefs of the Maya, also the same god of the fertile earth. The man above him with his leaping posture resembles emerging life. His face is reminiscent of that of the corn god, and for that reason he could be the incarnation of germinating nature. Authority and power were carried together with the ceremonial staff of the quartered universe, the cross, that is simultaneously an image of the world, time, and change of power. Lastly the bird Moan symbolizes death.[15]

The Prague professor Miloslav Stingl wore another pair of glasses:

One recognizes the figure of a young man, although obviously not an actual person, but a person—simply, the human race—is represented. A cross grows out of his body, which symbolizes the life-giving corn. Out of the corn leaves, entwined on both sides, double-headed snakes appear. . . . The body of the youth thus outgrows life, but itself rests on the face of death—the repulsive head of a fantastic animal, out of whose mouth protrude pointed tusks.[16]

The renowned Maya archaeologist Dr. Linda Schele sees that

In his burial chamber located deep below the cave temple in the heart of the pyramid, Pakal has recorded the deaths of the kings named in the temple hall above. In addition, he has them appear figuratively on the sidewalls of his sarcophagus as an orchard of ancestors emerging from crevices in the earth.[17]

In the course of the years—as is the case with a living science—new suggestions were voiced. They ranged from "earth monsters" to the "stylized whiskers of the weather god," from a "living cross" to a "broken rat's tail." Everyone discovered something different on the tombstone. Markus Eberl, one of the most recognized Maya specialists in recent times had this to say about the representation on the slab:

In some way, the inscription on the lid of K'inich Janaab Pakal's sarcophagus recounts what he should expect at death: following the call of his predecessors and ancestors, he entered the path to the underworld that his predecessors had already traveled. . . . The sarcophagus lid records a crucial moment on the journey to the afterlife. . . . The ruler rises from the skeletal jaws of the underworld in the form of the young corn god . . . and out of him grows a cross-forming world tree, that marks the way of the dead in the next world.[18]

In another work, Dr. Linda Schele refined her view of the tombstone:

The image on the sarcophagus lid shows Pakal's death and his travel to the underworld. The entire scene is framed through the band of sky with Kin ("day" or "sun") in the corner top right and with Abkal ("night" or "darkness") on the left. The cosmic event, which shows Pakal's journey in death, is the movement of the sun from east to west.[19]

It goes on like this for decades. Opinions, monsters, misunderstandings. Would you care for another expert opinion?

The scene on the slab is very similar to the representation on the Cross and Foliated Cross Temples. But this time, one person balances dangerously on the grotesque head of the earth monster. From the body of the man grows a cross-like tree, whose branches end in snake heads. Like in other Palenque sculptures, a wonderfully stylized bird overlooks the scene from its seat in the tree.[20]

The story of the interpretation remains alive. Thank God, I would like to add, because the Maya specialists are finally understanding more and more of the old glyphs. The absolute tops among Mayan epigraphers (deciphering) are David and

George Stuart. In the inscription, they read the story of the boy king Pakal up until his death. "The inscription ends with a record of death from Pakal's wife Ix Tz'akbu Ajaw in year 672, followed by the date of death of Pakal himself in 683."[21]

But the duo Stuart and Stuart also noted:

> Considered in its entirety, the sarcophagus can be viewed as a carefully put together model of the cosmos. . . . In the center of the symbols, one sees the reclining human figure of K'inich Janaab Pakal, surrounded by a complex cosmological presentation. The band of sky frames the entire scene and alludes to the things in heaven.

What earlier interpretations of the panel also saw as a "quetzal bird," Stuart and Stuart argue is a "supernatural bird." And if one agreed with the current opinion that King Pakal crashed into an earth monster, the actual doctrine sees it differently: King Pakal climbed out of the earth.

> This new meaning is clearly shown through the sun bowl, which is sometimes used in hieroglyphic texts with the sign "el" which means "ascend," "climb," or sometimes also "burn" and mostly in the word "el-l'in" ("east," "rising sun"). It is therefore reasonable that Pakal's position in the sun bowl is explicitly in the eastern direction, which means *Pakal ascends and he emerges from the earth with the sunrise* (emphasis added).[22]

And what is it with the ominous "tree of life" or "cross of life" that lies on Pakal's chest? Stuart and Stuart see in that an "abstract tree" that is often described by experts as a "world tree" because of its cross-like form, although this does not mean

Figure 207

anything sensible. "For the Maya, trees always had a very complex and important cosmological meaning."

Critical in the newest interpretation of the tombstone of
Palenque is the conclusion that Pakal did not go to any underworld, but rather went toward the heavens.

Exactly this has been my concern for the past fifty years.
Understandably, the "cross of life" or "tree of life" does not represent any kind of rocket (figure 207): but it is about something
misunderstood from the cargo school. If even the experts can
begin with such vague concepts as "tree of life" and "cross of life,"
might other viewpoints also be possible? Linda Schele identifies
the "world tree with heavenly birds" and a "Kan cross water-lily
monster."[23] The panel also contains a "band of sky" (Schele), and
both ribbed curves on the right and left growing out of the "tree
of life" are "snub-nosed dragons" (Schele). Elsewhere, I also read

Figure 208

that it depicts broken rats' tails. Now, the Maya archaeologists and epigraphers have certainly done outstanding work. Oddballs or followers of any conspiracy theories are not included. They try to be honest and explain with much expertise that which is difficult to understand. Yet ultimately, all thought is subject to reason. And this changes from generation to generation.

The fact remains that King Pakal is represented in a unique posture. He sits forward inclined to the east, toward the rising sun—and this according to the latest reading, so as not to fall between the canines of an "earth monster." He flies away from the earth (figure 208). Two fingers of his upper hand are together, as if they were making a fine adjustment. On his lower hand, one can recognize the four bent fingers of the back of the hand. They turn something. With that, the professional opinion of father and son Stuart is that the panel can be "considered in its entirety . . . as a carefully put together model of the cosmos."

In cargo-cult thinking, no perfect technological representations exist because the forefathers, who saw something technological, could not make heads or tails of it. They did not have a clue
about what they saw, not to mention their descendants centuries
or millennia later. Then divine articles were handed down, which
had some amazing effects: they could fly, shoot, make light, cause
tremors, and obviously also lift up selected people. For people
of the Stone Age, a car with headlights and radiator was viewed
with bright eyes and gaping mouth. These encounters with foreign objects migrate indelibly into the brains of the people. Too
impressive, too formidable, too foreign, too "divine," too powerful
were the confrontations of the people of the day with such foreign technology to ever be erased from their memories. All the
more so since the priests continuously drummed the unexplainable into their people, and the artists translated the same into
stuccoworks, statues, and temples. Something like this survives
ineradicably from generation to generation. Today's living religions demonstrate this. Despite history books and Gospels, we do
not know what actually happened during Jesus's time. But we also
believe after two thousand years in the nonsense of immaculate
conception, ascending to heaven, raising from the dead, and so on.
It was not very different millennia before. Our technologically
clueless Stone Age people did not realize this—but it impressed
them enormously. Logically, their descendants understood even
less—although the gods, together with their objects, were further
revered. The mystery remains a mystery. Everything divine is mysterious. This is called cargo cult. With this premise in the back of
my mind, I recognize many misunderstood cult objects in Maya
Land, including the tombstone of Palenque. Whereby it does not
matter in the cargo view whether the image is viewed horizontally
or vertically (figure 209).

Figure 209

We devoutly accept words from the Maya world that happen to sound scientific but are nonetheless detached from reality. What do the following phrases mean: double-headed snake bands, quartered sun monsters, jaws of the underworld, world tree, square dragon nose, supernatural bird, Kan-cross soul monster, snub-nosed dragons, and so on—all referring to the tombstone? A swelling of ideas that only make sense in a very specific model, and only then with a portion of devout faith. The argument for the "snub-nosed dragons" emerged in other Maya temples, as did the "quartered monster" or "supernatural bird," and therefore the current view is compelling, and does not offend. Why? Because the interpretations went in the wrong direction from the beginning. The reading of a glyph must not be the meaning of the glyph. A "light year" is not the electricity bill for a year.

Pakal, the buried king of Palenque, was not a legitimate heir to the throne. Therefore—according to the doctrinal view—his family invented a story in order to present him as a heavenly ruler to the people. So Pakal became the reincarnation of earlier gods. His son Chan-Bahlum solidified this claim. He deified his father and described the creation of earth on his pyramid. Necessarily, the father Pakal as a descendant of the gods had an important role to play. Since this view is so and cannot be read from the glyphs of Palenque, no other conclusions can be drawn from it. I would like to bring up a modest objection: Why did other cultures (Tibet, Egypt, India, Babylon, and so on) from the same crazy time as the Maya pass on traditions of "sons of gods"? Did the royal dynasties of our predecessors worldwide suffer the same flight of fancy? Or was there somewhere in the global pantheon of all gods a common ground that has escaped us?

All temples of the Buddhist culture know the stupa form. Whether in India, Indonesia, Myanmar, Thailand, and elsewhere, stupas are ubiquitous. For Westerners a stupa looks like a bell with a handle (figure 210). In Buddhism a stupa has different meanings, one of which is that it is a small vehicle to the larger world of the gods. Stupas are therefore not empty (figure 211). The young Buddha sits inside and performs ritual movements with his hands, which connect his small vehicle with the larger heavenly vehicle of the gods. Nothing different from Pakal in his "cosmic setting" on the other side of the globe. How about a new science? Central American Indology.

Figure 210

Figure 211

Could it possibly be that some things in this wide world are much more connected and even simpler when we smart-alecks think together?

Notes

PROLOGUE. LETTER TO MY READERS

1. Urs Bitterli, *Die Wilden und die Zivilisierten* (Munich, 1976).
2. Christopher Columbus, *Das Bordbuch von 1492 und andere Aufzeichnungen*, ed. R. Grün (Tübingen, 1970).
3. Victor von Hagen, *Die Wüstenkönigreiche Perus* (Bergisch Gladbach, 1979).
4. Jules Verne, *Die grossen Seefahrer und Entdecker* (Zurich, 1974).

1. CARGO CULTS WITH CONSEQUENCES

1. Erich von Däniken, *Der Götter-Schock* (Munich, 1992).
2. Guglielmo Guariglia, "Prophetismus und Heilserwartungsbewegungen als völkerkundliches und religionsgeschichtliches Problem," in *Wiener Beiträge zur Kulturgeschichte und Linguistik* 13 (Vienna: Ferdinand Berger, 1959).
3. Frank Hurley, *Perlen und Wilde* (Leipzig, 1926).
4. Diego Garcia de Palacio, *Carta dirigida al Rey de España* (Honduras and San Salvador, 1576).
5. Morley quoted in Rafael Girare, *Die ewigen Mayas* (Zurich, 1969).
6. G. R. Josyer, *Vymaanika-Shaastra or Science of Aeronautics* (Mysore, India, 1973); Dileep Kumar Kanjilal, *Vimanas in Ancient India* (Calcutta, 1985).
7. Erich von Däniken, *Grüsse aus der Steineit* (Rottenburg, 2010).

8. Erich von Däniken, *Der Götter-Schock* (Munich, 1992); Erich von Däniken, *Habe ich mich geirrt?* (Munich, 1991).

9. Karl Friedrich Geldner, *Der Rig-Veda*, part 2 (Wiesbaden, 1951).

10. "Kebra Nagest: Die Herrlichkeit der Könige," in *Abhandlungen der philosophisch-philologischen Klasse der Königlich-Bayerischen Akademie der Wissenschaften* 23, ed. Carl Bezold (Munich, 1905).

11. "Das Buch Henoch," in *Apokryphen und Pseudigraphen des Alten Testaments*, vol. 2, trans. Emil Kautsch (Tübingen, 1900); Paul Riessler, *Altjüdisches Schrifttum ausserhalb der Bibel* (Augsburg, 1928).

12. *Die Heilige Schrift des Alten und des Neuen Testaments* (Stuttgart, 1972).

13. R. O. Faulkner, *The Ancient Egyptian Pyramid Texts* (Oxford, 1969).

14. Heinrich Brugsch, *Die Sage von der geflügelten Sonnenscheibe nach altägyptischen Quellen* (Göttingen, 1870).

2. PLACES TO HONOR THE GODS

1. Bernardino de Sahagún, *Historia general de las cocas de la Nueva España* (Madrid, n.d.).

2. Ibid.

3. Eduard Seler, *Gesammelte Abhandlungen zur Amerikanischen Sprach- und Altertumskunde*, vol. 4 (Graz, 1961).

4. Laurette Séjourné, *Pansiamento y religion en el México Antig.* (Mexico, 1957).

5. Constance Irwin, *Fair Gods and Stone Faces* (London, 1964).

6. Hugh Harleston, "A Mathematical Analysis of Teotiguacán," in *XLI International Congress of Americanists* (Mexico, 1974).

7. Paul H. Krannich, *Teufelswerk: Ein Sachbuch über exakte Naturwissenschaft in der Steinzeit* (Norderstedt: BOD, 2010).

8. Wolfgang Feix, "Eine Botschaft von Alpha Centauri? Die Grosse Pyramide von Giseh und die Sonnenpyramide von Teotihuacán als Träger kosmolinguistischen Daten," in *Kosmische Spuren,* ed. Erich von Däniken (Munich, 1988).

9. Walter Lehmann, *Die Geschichte der Königsreiche von Colhuacan und Mexico* (Stuttgart/Berlin, 1938).

10. Irene Nicholson, *Mexican and Central American Mythology* (London and New York, 1967).

11. Ferdinand Anders, *Das Pantheon der Maya* (Graz, 1963).

12. Arnost Dittrich, *Der Planet Venus und seine Behandlung im Dresdener Maya-Kodex* (Berlin: Prussian Academy of Sciences, 1937); Michael Rowan-Robinson, "Mayan Astronomy," *New Scientist*, October 18, 1979.

13. Robert Henseling, "Das Alter der Maya-Astronomie," in: *Forschungen und Fortschnitte. Nachrichtenblatt der deutschen Wissenschaft und Technik* 25, nos. 3 and 4, (February 1949).

14. Ralph L. Roys, *The Book of Chilam-Balam of Chumayel* (Washington, D.C.: Carnegie Institution, 1933).

15. Eugene R. Craine and Reginald C. Reindorp, *The Codex Perez and the Book of Chilam-Balam of Mani* (Norman: University of Oklahoma Press, 1979).

16. Charles-Etienne Brasseur de Bourbourg, *Histoire des nations civilićees du Mexique et de l'Amerique-Centrale*, 6 vols. (Paris, 1857–1859).

17. Leonhard Schultze-Jena, *Popol Vuh: Das heilige Buch der Quiché-Indianer von Guatemala* (Stuttgart/Berlin, 1944).

18. Otto Apelt, *Platons Dialoge Timaios und Kritias* (Leipzig, 1922).

19. Herodotus, *Buch der Historien*, vol. 2, chaps. 141 and 142.

20. Plato, *Timaeus*, trans. Benjamin Jowett (Oxford, 1892).

21. Bernardino de Sahagún, *Wahrsagerei, Himmelskunde und Kalendar der alten Azteken*, trans. Leonhard Schulze-Jena (Stuttgart, 1950).

22. Ibid.

23. Frederic V. Grunfeld, *Spiele der Welt: Tlachtli* (Zurich: Swiss Committee for UNICEF, n.d.).

24. Diego de Landa, *Yucatán Before and After the Conquest*, trans. William Gates (New York, 1978).

25. Worchester M. Makemson, *The Book of the Jaguar Priest: A Translation of the Book of Chilam Balam of Tizimin with Commentary* (New York, 1951).

3. NONSTOP CURIOSITIES

1. John L. Stephens, *Incidents of Travel in Central America, Chiapas and Yucatán*, 2 vols. (New York, 1843).

2. Paul Riesler, "Die Apokryphe des Abraham," in *Altjüdisches Schtifttum ausserhalf ber Bibel* (Augsburg, 1928).

3. Wilfried Westphal, *Die Maya: Volk im Schatten seiner Väter* (Munich, 1977).

4. Richard E. Blanton, *Monte Albán: Settlement Patterns at the Ancient Zapotec Capital* (New York: Academic Press, 1978).

5. J. Marcus and K. Flannery, *Zapotec Civilization: How Urban Society Evolved in Mexico's Oaxaca Valley* (London, 1996).

6. Peter Buck, *Vikings of the Pacific* (Chicago, 1972).

7. Edward Smith Craighill Handy, *The Native Culture in Marquesas*, Bulletin no. 9 (Honolulu: B. P. Bishop Museum, 1923).

8. Edward Smith Craighill Handy, *Polynesian Religion*, Bulletin no. 34 (Honolulu: B. P. Bishop Museum, 1927).

9. Johannes C. Andersen, *Myths and Legends of the Polynesians* (1928; repr., New York: Dover, 2011).

10. Alaima Talu et al. *Kiribati: Aspects of History* (Tarawa, Kiribati, 1979).

11. Pedro Simon, *Noticias Historiales de las Conquistas de Tierra Firma en las Indias Occidentales* (Bogota, Colombia, 1890).

12. Paul Frischauer, *Es steht geschrieben.* (Munich 1967).

13. Doris Stone, "A Preliminary Investigation of the Flood Plain of the Rio Grande de Térraba, Costa Rica," *American Antiquity* 9, no. 1 (July 1943).

4. KING PAKAL'S ASCENSION

1. Erich von Däniken, *Der Tag an dem die Götter kamen* (Munich, 1984).

2. Brian M. Fagan, *Die vergrabene Sonne* (Munich, 1979).

3. Stephens, *Incidents of Travel in Central America*.

4. M. E. Kampen, *The Religion of the Maya* (Leiden, The Netherlands: E. J. Brill, 1981).

5. Herbert Willhelmy, *Welt und Umwelt der Maya* (Munich, 1981).

6. H. Berlin, "The Palenque Triad," *Journal de la Société der Américanistes* 52, no. 1, 1963.

7. David Stuart and George E. Stuart, *Palenque: Eternal City of the Maya* (London, 2008).

8. Ibid.

9. Diodorus Siculus, *Bibliotheca Historica* (Stuttgart, 1866).

10. H. von Pessl, *Das Chronologische System Manetho's* (Leipzig, 1878).

11. Stuart and Stuart, *Palenque: Eternal City of the Maya*.

12. Alberto Ruz Lhuiller, "The Mystery of the Temple of the Inscriptions," trans. J. Alden Mason, *Archaeology* 6, no. 1 (March 1953): 3–11.

13. Ibid.

14. Willhelmy, *Welt und Umwelt der Maya*.

15. Pierre Ivanoff, *Maya: Monumente grosser Kulturen* (Luxembourg, 1974).

16. Miroslav Stingl, *Den Maya auf der Spur* (Leipzig, 1971).

17. Linda Schele and David Freidel, *Die unbekannte Welt der Maya* (Munich, 1990).

18. Markus Eberl, "Tod und Seelenvorstellungen," in *Maya: Gotkönige im Regenwald*, ed. Nikolai Grube (Cologne, 2000).

19. Linda Schele and Mary Ellen Miller, *The Blood of Kings* (Fort Worth, Tex.: Kimbell Art Museum, 1986).

20. Merle Greene, Robert L. Rands, and John A. Graham, *Maya Sculpture from the Southern Lowlands, the Highlands and Pacific Piedmont, Guatemala, Mexico, Honduras* (Berkeley, Calif.: Lederer, Street & Zeus, 1972).

21. Stuart and Stuart, *Palenque: Eternal City of the Maya*.

22. Ibid.

23. Schele and Freidel, *Die unbekannte Welt der Maya*.

Image Sources

Figure 1: Illustration from Jules Verne, *Die grossen Seefahrer und Entdecker* (Zurich 1974).

Figures 2 and 3: From the movie *Erinnerungen an die Zukunft*. Archive EvD.

Figures 4 and 5: *Musée de l'Homme*, Paris.

Figure 7: Hurley, Frank: *Perlen und Wilde*, (Leipzig, 1926).

Figure 8: NASA, PAO, Washington, DC.

Figure 19: Fátima children.

Figures 51 and 52: From the movie *Erinerungen an die Zukunft*, Archive EvD.

Figures 90 and 91: Tatjana Ingold, CH-Solothurn.

Figure 95: *Instituto Nacional de Anthropologia e Historia,* Mexico City.

Figure 103: Computer image of Ralf Lange, CH-Zuchwil.

Figures 110 and 111: Rudolf Eckhardt, Berlin.

Figures 121 and 122: SAT I TV Series *Auf den Spuren der All-Mächtigen*, 1993.

Figure 154 and 155: Image gallery in government palace of Mexico City, Photo: EvD.

Figure 189: Doris Z. Stone, Guatemala City, 1944.

Figures 125, 127, 193–202: Mathias Lang, Kandern, Germany.

ALL OTHER IMAGES

Erich von Däniken, Archive EvD: Copyright © Erich von Däniken, CH-3803 Beatenberg, Switzerland.

Index